Ovid

Classical Poetry

Volumes published in this Brill Research Perspectives title are listed at *brill.com/rpcp*

Ovid

By

Francesca K.A. Martelli

BRILL

LEIDEN | BOSTON

This paperback book edition is simultaneously published as issue 2.1 (2020) of *Classical Poetry*,
DOI:10.1163/25892649-12340003

Library of Congress Control Number: 2020950955

Typeface for the Latin, Greek, and Cyrillic scripts: "Brill". See and download: brill.com/brill-typeface.

ISBN 978-90-04-44976-3 (paperback)
ISBN 978-90-04-45006-6 (e-book)

Contents

Ovid

Francesca K.A. Martelli
University of California, Los Angeles
fmartelli@humnet.ucla.edu

Abstract

In this volume, Francesca Martelli outlines some of the main contours of recent, current and future research on Ovid. Her study looks back to the rehabilitation of Ovid's oeuvre in the 1980s, and considers the post-modern aesthetic prerogatives and post-structuralist theoretical concerns that drove the critical recuperation of his poetry throughout that decade and in the decades that followed. But it also looks forward, by considering how the themes of this poet's oeuvre answer to a variety of new materialist concerns that are now gaining currency in the humanities and social sciences. It highlights the ecopoetic sensibility of the *Metamorphoses*, for example, and unpacks the environmental narratives that this poem yields when read in dialogue with the discourses of critical posthumanism. And it closes by considering the hauntological aesthetics of Ovid's exile poetry as a comment on the effects of the principate on time, space, media, and art.

Keywords

Ovid – post-structuralism – desire – posthumanism – environment – nature – materialism – exile – media – hauntology

1 Introduction: Ovid, a Poet between Paradigms

A cherished trope of much recent Ovidian criticism maintains that the resurgence of critical interest in this author from the late 1980s was indebted to an affinity between his poetics and the hallmarks of post-modernism.[1] Unlike

---

1 One of the most overt statements to this effect is that of Myers 1999, which presents Terry Eagleton's description of post-modernism (in Eagleton 1996a) as an apposite description of

Virgil, whose poetry had consistently maintained a canonical status since antiquity, an appreciation of Ovid's literary output has fluctuated widely throughout the history of his reception.[2] When Ovid, who had been widely removed from school and university curricula for a century or more, began in the late twentieth century to attract a critical attention not seen since the Renaissance, scholars noted the parallels between the most distinctive characteristics of this author's writing and the stock-in-trade of late twentieth century style: eclectic in its juxtaposition of high and low genres and deliberately derivative in its cultural debts and influences, Ovid's poetry advertises its belatedness in ways that conform to an idiom defined by the 'post-'. Likewise, this poet's interest in rhetoric and in the verbal illusions through which phenomena are made to materialize out of the very surface of language speaks to a post-modern distrust of essentialist claims to truth and reality in favour of the discourses that produce those claims. Add to this Ovid's anti-closural, anti-teleological take on narrative and history, and his characteristic view of the human subject as plural, fragmentary, and in flux, and it is not hard to see why recent generations of scholars have found in his work a mirror of the post-modern. But where are we to locate this poet, in critical terms, in 2020? The answer that we give to this question will rely on what we make of the currency of those discourses that fuelled his critical resurgence, and whether we can make his poetry answer to the new discourses that are poised to displace them.

Post-modernism, and its kindred movement post-structuralism, are notoriously hard to escape. Both discourses position themselves as responses to movements (modernism/structuralism, related but different) that came before. And the longevity of both owes much to the seemingly infinite chain of supplementation enabled by the 'post-', the logic of which is to seek an endless process of replication, one that wants to claim every movement that comes after, however different, as iterations of the same – further gestures of supplementation. And yet there are critical movements alive in the humanities and social sciences today, which are resistant to being subsumed into post-structuralism's broad church, and which are indebted to distinct, even oppositional, theoretical

---

Ovid's literary tastes and principles. The decision to quote Eagleton's description of post-modernism is in some ways a surprising one, since his hostility to the movement is well known (cf. e.g. Eagleton 1996b), and may be discerned underlying the description of his that she quotes. Rimell 2019, 2–5 offers a more recent and comprehensive survey of the explicit links that scholars have drawn between post-modernism and Ovidian poetry.

2   Fränkel 1945 suggests that the nineteenth century marked the nadir of Ovid's critical appreciation (a low-point matched only by his standing at the time of Fränkel's writing). See Vance 1988 for a partial reassessment of this view. The essays collected in Martindale 1988 still offer a serviceable overview of the history of Ovid's reception since the Middle Ages.

positions and traditions. Critical posthumanism, for example, seeks to displace
the human from the centre of western thought by locating her in complex networks of biological, technological, and economic exchange and interaction.[3]
In emphasising the extent to which the human subject's thought and actions
are dependent on, and determined by, material forces beyond her control, this
critical movement owes a significant debt to older materialist philosophies,
such as Marxism and Freudian psychoanalysis, which similarly stress the sub-
jection of individual human consciousness to material systems (economic or
organic).[4] The emphasis in these philosophies on the material conditions of
life and being stands in friction with the post-structuralist desire to see reality as never anything more than a rhetorical effect. So too for the movements
allied with critical post-humanism: materialist ontologies displace the cog-
nizant human subject by situating her against non-human objects of greater
power and longevity,[5] while affect theory de-privileges human cognition by
showing what it owes to the body and the senses.[6] All these new materialisms
share a dissatisfaction with the textualist and linguistic foundations of post-
structuralism, and seek to reposition our intellectual priorities by focusing on
the material dimensions of being that post-structuralism disavowed.

The analysis of Ovid's literary productions may currently be situated in, or
between, either one of these critical arenas. For while most scholarship on
this poet's oeuvre continues in its habitual vein, few would deny how readily
that oeuvre lends itself to the posthumanist and/or new materialist discourses
that have lately irrupted across the humanities. Ovid was once described by
Hermann Fränkel as 'a poet between two worlds',[7] a description that subsequent

---

3   Wolfe 2010, xv borrows Lyotard's paradoxical rendering of the post-modern for his own for-
    mulation of posthumanism as a movement that comes both before and after humanism:
    "Before in the sense that it names the embodiment and embeddedness of the human being
    in not just its biological but also its technological world ... all of which comes before that his-
    torically specific thing called the human that Foucault's archaeology excavates. But it comes
    after in the sense that posthumanism names a historical moment in which the decentering
    of the human by its imbrication in technical, medical, informatic, and economic networks is
    increasingly impossible to ignore ..."
4   This is why, as Alaimo 2010, 6 notes, contemporary theorists out to recuperate 'the "stuff"
    of matter', have either situated themselves within a tradition of philosophers, from Spinoza
    to Deleuze, that represents a counter-tradition to the linguistic turn; or have premised their
    work on re-readings of theorists at the heart of post-structuralism. The attempt by Wolfe
    2010, 3–30 to relate various works of Derrida on the system of writing to the systems theory
    of Luhmann 1995 may be viewed as an example of the latter practice.
5   Morton 2013; and Harman 2018.
6   Gregg and Seigworth 2010, 5.
7   Fränkel 1945. Both Rosati 1983, 95–97 and Hardie 2002a, 28 resuscitate Fränkel's phrase and
    put it in the service of their own respective critical projects. Fielding 2017, 1–2 returns to

critics have reclaimed for their own view of Ovid's place in literary and other histories. But the label also offers an apposite description of his place within and between the shifting tectonic plates of our own critical universe. In this survey, I offer an overview of some of the scholarship conducted on his poetry under the sign of post-structuralism (or its various sub-fields), and lay out what I think the new materialisms (or one particular variant of them) might bring to the study of his texts. The latter approach arguably lends itself most readily to the fluid ontologies of the *Metamorphoses*, so readers interested in this critical direction should go directly to the second section of my discussion of this text, where they will find my thoughts on this set out. The readiness with which Ovid's epic poem responds to the ecological discourses that gather under the broad rubric of the new materialisms makes it answer to some of the most pressing existential issues of our time. Ovidian frivolity was celebrated by the post-modern sensibility of the late-twentieth century. So too, many of the new materialisms are haunted by the grittier political import of their older materialist predecessors.[8] Materialist approaches to the environment, by contrast, have a clear political resonance and make the *Metamorphoses* read quite differently to the text that we are accustomed to viewing along post-structuralist lines, in which landscape only ever exists at the level of metapoetry.

This volume is, then, driven by the desire to recuperate Ovid as a poet who speaks to the political questions and conditions of our own era. While such questions are hardly absent from the post-modern appraisals of this poet's oeuvre, they are generally limited to issues that touch on the politics of identity, above all sexuality and gender – important questions, which are the subject of a brilliant review essay published recently by Victoria Rimell.[9] But they are also open to criticisms commonly laid at post-modernism regarding the preoccupation with the self that this movement brings to the fore. (The prevalence of Narcissus in such readings makes them vulnerable to parody from this perspective.) Nor do they exhaust the question of the political in Ovid. One reaction to the political vacuum left by scholarship in this vein would be to follow the approaches taken by cultural materialists, who compensate for it by stressing the hegemonic structures on which much ancient literature is premised, and who argue that ignoring

---

Fränkel's original conception of the phrase, which identifies Ovid as a bridge between the pagan world of antiquity and Christianity, by focusing on Ovid's reception in the transition to Christianity that took place in Late Antiquity.

8   Cf. Nersessian 2017 on the relative political vacuity of certain modes of New Materialist discourse. See also Hall 2018 for a Classicist's take on the battle between materialisms, old and new.

9   Rimell 2019.

(and/or forgiving) these structures is a way of colluding with their strategies of domination.[10] Ovid tends not to fare well in these readings, and while I have learned much from them, I do not believe that they capture in full the ideological critique that this poet's aesthetic choices are capable of bringing to bear on the hegemony of which he forms part.

Another approach would be to take our cue from the political criticisms lodged at post-modernism itself, the most famous of which, by Frederic Jameson, disparages the movement as an expression of the cultural logic of late capitalism.[11] Jameson singles out the apolitical nature of the post-modernist appropriation of consumerist culture as the central target of his Marxist critique, which also takes in the aesthetic consequences of this appropriation: its depthlessness, weakening of historicity, and the 'waning of affect' that accompanies these effects. Jameson's objections to the post-modern aesthetic resemble many of the older criticisms that used to be lodged at Ovid's poetry (his shallowness, for example, or lack of sincerity), and may seem a little outmoded as a result of this. Nevertheless, in relating this aesthetic to the political and/or economic structures of his day, his approach points one way toward rethinking the political charge of Ovid's writing.

An alternative way of modelling the relationship between the economic and cultural dimensions of late capitalism is proffered by that pillar of post-structuralism, Jacques Derrida, who, in one of his later political writings, elaborates his own version of Marxism in his appraisal of the way in which it 'haunts' the system that won out.[12] In Derrida's hands, the media apparatuses that accompany late capitalism are symptomatic of the economic system on which they are predicated; but rather than disparaging them on this grounds, Derrida puts them in the service of elucidating the logic of that very system. Derrida's coinage 'hauntology' has been picked up by contemporary music critics to describe a pop movement that comments on the derivative digital music of the twenty-first century, and the consumerist culture on which it is premised, by resampling it to uncanny effect.[13] In my section on Ovid's exile poetry, I suggest that we can profitably draw on their approach to the politics of culture to unpack the political resonance of the poet's negative aesthetic choices and techniques in exile. The ideological contexts for which *Spectres of*

---

10   Habinek 1998 is still the most trenchant example of this broad position. See also Richlin 2014 for a more specific focus on how these hegemonic structures serve to repress women.

11   Jameson 1991 (discussed on pp. 11–12 below). Eagleton 1996b critiques post-modernism from a similar Marxist stance.

12   Derrida 1994.

13   Cf. esp. Fisher 2014; and Tanner 2016 (whose work is discussed on p. 73 below).

Marx and Ovid's exile poetry were written are clearly very different. Yet each is predicated on the existence of an alternative political and discursive system (Marxism, on the one hand, and the Republic, on the other), the memory of which it cannot entirely repress, because of the residual traces that these alternatives leave in the dominant system as gaps or contradictions. My view of the political in the exile poetry focuses not on what Ovid says about the principate, but rather on what his reflections about how media operate in this strange time and space reveal about the historical conditions of his moment of writing.

My study thus traces a course through the post-structuralist recuperation of Ovidian poetry in the past thirty years (analysed above all in the early amatory works, and in my initial survey of work on the *Metamorphoses*);[14] through the recent move to surpass this discourse in favour of a paradigm that accommodates the material side of Ovid's poetry (in my reading of the *Metamorphoses*); and which finally moves beyond phenomenal matter to embrace a more politically charged materialism in the exile poetry. In this way, I use the structure of his oeuvre to shape my own narrative about the way these discourses relate to one another, and suggest that this narrative is facilitated to some considerable extent by the shape of his literary career. The mutual implications of this argument make it doubtless as narcissistic as any claim to find in Ovid the mirror of the post-modern. But they also highlight how readily his poetry responds to shifting critical positions. As ever, his oeuvre helps to articulate the changing context against which we read it, and offers a political critique of the conditions that necessitate such change at the same time. In this sense, Ovid remains a poet caught between two (or more) worlds.

2   **Gender, Sexuality, and Desire in the *Amores, Ars Amatoria,* and *Heroides***

Ovid's literary career begins with a series of experiments in the genre of love elegy, which aim to probe the limits of this genre and subject it to various

---

14   Because I am primarily interested in tracing a narrative of Ovidian scholarship through its engagement with critical theory, the bulk of the scholarship that I survey in this study is Anglophone, simply because critical theory looms larger in Anglo-American scholarship on Ovid than it does in scholarship in other languages. Scholars who do not represent this tradition will doubtless baulk at its procedures of exclusion (cf. Holzberg 2018). But see Kenney 2001 for arguments about the pragmatic need to cut some kind of exclusionary path through the current volume of scholarship on this author. That need is particularly pressing in a brief survey like this one.

procedures of hybridization and expansion.[15] These early works have benefited substantially from the broader critical turns that Latin love elegy has undergone in the past thirty years or so, but have also attracted additional discourses in keeping with their more expansive interests. The discourse of desire that love elegy seeks to encode responds to a number of post-structuralist cruxes: Lacanian and Freudian models of desire have been put in the service of unpacking the erotic charge of Latin love elegy in general, and of Ovid's particular brand of it in particular, while the patently discursive status of Ovid's treatment of *amor* in both the *Amores* and the *Ars Amatoria* has been systematically plotted and deconstructed. The construction of gender has been another *topos* of recent scholarship on elegy, not least the *Amores*. But gender receives further attention in Ovid's early erotic oeuvre both because of the way in which the poet exposes the objectified (and victimized) status of the female in elegy's masculine fantasies in texts like the *Ars Amatoria*, while at the same time giving voice to the female in texts like the *Heroides*. The *Heroides*, which take the form of verse epistles, add to these critical approaches an interest in epistolarity, a (sub-)literary mode that plays a key explanatory role in Lacan's view of desire and subjectivity. In many ways, the critical tenets and biases of recent scholarship on Ovid's amatory works are representative of the scholarship on the rest of his oeuvre.

Of all the love elegists, Ovid's critical estimation suffered for some time as a result of his coming last, a final position that is implicitly taken as a failure of his own making. The reason for this becomes clear when we consider the (often notionally appreciative) terms in which his relationship with his predecessors is couched: between them, Gallus, Propertius, and Tibullus are held to have worked creatively with the conventions of the genre they were forging from within it. Ovid, by contrast, observes the system that love elegy constitutes in the hands of these earlier practitioners, and sets out to parody it. This is explicitly the case for the *Ars Amatoria*, the didactic format of which makes the systemic nature of elegy's discourse explicit,[16] but it is also no less true for the *Amores*, which suffered particularly from the label of parody that came to attach to it.[17] To those readers habituated to ideas of hypertextuality (of which

---

15   As recent scholarship (e.g. Thorsen 2014, 1–38) has emphasised, it is very difficult to plot these works into a stable chronological order, given the process of revision that Ovid advertises for them. For purposes of argumentative ease only, in this section I will treat the *Amores* first, followed by the *Ars Amatoria*, and finally the *Heroides*.

16   Kennedy 1993, 65.

17   Boyd 1997, 10–11 lists the number of earlier critics who labelled the *Amores*, with greater or lesser degrees of distaste, as parody. As she points out, this tradition of scholarship culminates in the monograph of Morgan 1977.

parody is identified by Genette as an important example),[18] it may seem odd to find the *Amores'* status as parody treated as grounds for its disparagement. But as Boyd points out, underlying many of the earlier appraisals of the parodic qualities of this work is an implicit judgment about its refusal to conjure the romanticism and illusions of sincerity, which are assumed to be a defining feature of Latin elegy.[19] It therefore took the efforts of textualist scholars working on Propertius, such as Maria Wyke, who exploded the idea of love elegy's inscription of sincere romantic passion, by demonstrating (for example) that the elegiac *puella* is a patent literary construction,[20] in order to begin recuperating Ovid's detached treatment of *amor* as a legitimate elegiac exercise.[21]

This process of recuperation initially took two main courses: on the one hand came the attempt made by Duncan Kennedy to position Ovid as firmly at home among the elegists by explicating the themes and stories of Latin love elegy as part of a lover's discourse.[22] This enterprise takes the love (and lovers) of Latin elegy as a test case for some much wider questions about representation and reality, terms that appear to operate in opposition to one another in the hands of earlier scholars of erotic elegy, but which, as Kennedy shows, rely on each other in order to create meaning within their own discursive fields. Kennedy's discussion of this issue carries much wider implications for the way in which we think of and write about the past,[23] but homes in on love because of its value as a theme that appears universal, but which is in fact thoroughly caught up in the discourses, perspectives, and determining interests of history. Kennedy uses this tension to deconstruct a number of discourses that touch on love and love elegy in some way: the 'meaning' of love, far from being trans-historical, turns out to be as historically and subjectively situated as the meanings of other so-called essentialist terms, such as gender and sexuality, terms that participate in discourses with long histories.[24] Kennedy lays out the deconstructive reflexes of their histories, and demonstrates how they

---

18   Genette 1997, 10–19 on parody as a paradigmatic example of 'literature in the second degree'.

19   Boyd 1997, 11. Cf. also Kennedy 1993, 66: "The position represented as 'Ovidian' is surprising only insofar as the one represented as 'Propertian' is presumed to speak the truth about love." This view had some proponents decades earlier (cf. e.g. Allen 1950).

20   Cf. e.g. Wyke 1987a and 1987b; and Wyke 1989a and 1989b (now all collected in Wyke 2002).

21   Cf. e.g. Wyke 1989b; and Keith 1994, for samples of work on the construction of the *puellae* of the *Amores*.

22   Kennedy 1993.

23   Kennedy 1993, 7–12 offers an especially probing set of insights into historicism's reliance on representations, textual or otherwise.

24   Kennedy 1993, 24–45 (Chapter 3: 'Getting Down to Essentials').

are already deconstructed in antiquity, frequently by the elegists themselves.[25] But his own deconstructive insight is to show how these histories nevertheless rely on analytical terms (e.g. sexuality and gender) that project themselves as being universally and trans-historically valid in order for them to remain (sic.) legible and/or meaningful to us now. As Kennedy puts it, 'Representing the past as fundamentally different involves projecting it at some level, however occluded, as also fundamentally the same.'[26]

Much of Kennedy's book emphasises the similarities between the past and present of erotic discourse, as the conventional positions assumed by the poet-lover of Latin love elegy are shown to resemble techniques and positions advocated in Barthes' *Fragments d'un discours amoreux*, where the line between art and life, erotics and aesthetics is similarly deconstructed. Unsurprisingly, Ovid's *Amores*, a work that deconstructs these oppositions in its very title,[27] and which openly seeks to explode the fictions of authentic love on which elegy is premised throughout, takes centre stage in this discussion. Kennedy notes, for example, the preponderance of dramatic monologues that appear in this collection,[28] and suggests how such poems, in their rhetoricity, fulfil the advice administered at *Ars.* 1.611, that in order to be the lover you need to play the role of one. This enacts much the 'same' insight that Barthes promotes, that 'there is a lover's discourse and we construct ourselves as amorous subjects within it.'[29] Many of the precise rhetorical terms and tropes of elegiac discourse may be specific to Roman culture (e.g. *milita amoris*, exemplified – or parodied – in *Am.* 1.9).[30] But Kennedy's point is that the figurative language of love has ever brought its discourses into a range of other discourses, from warfare to finance, that might seem to have little to do with the erotic, yet which it relies on in order to make its activities and relationships expressible.[31] One cannot isolate

---

25   Cf. e.g. Kennedy 1993, 28–34, on how the elegists deconstruct gender distinctions.

26   Kennedy 1993, 40–41.

27   Kennedy 1993, 82. The title of Ovid's *Amores* is thought to reproduce the title of Gallus' collection of elegies.

28   Cf. e.g. the discussion of *Am.* 1.14 in Kennedy 1993, 71–73.

29   Kennedy 1993, 65 glossing Barthes 1979, 136.

30   Kennedy 1993, 54–56, for discussion of elegy's use of the language of warfare. His discussion of the promotion of sexual violence or (metaphorical) 'violence' at *Ars.* 1.673–674 may get to the heart of the alibi-in-metaphor constructed by the *magister amoris* for himself and his pupils, but does little to address the perspective of their female target. When does the person who feels the effects of violence (whether psychological, verbal or physical) ever experience it as metaphor?

31   Kennedy 1993, 56–57 discusses the use of financial language in the terminology for orgasm in Victorian England, which, he argues, relates to the key Victorian value of thrift. Cf. also now Kennedy 2012; and O'Rourke 2018.

sex or 'love', these most seemingly essential activities, from anything else, and in this the elegists bear out the same deconstructive message as Barthes. Ovid, in reflecting on this aspect of elegy with particular self-consciousness, brings its discourses especially close to the post-structuralist interests for which Kennedy was writing.

Another significant route taken by scholars seeking to shake off the derivative connotations of the *Amores'* status as a parody of the tradition of erotic elegy that precedes it was to demonstrate how far its intertextual range extends beyond erotic elegy, and how far its hypertextual techniques range beyond 'mere' parody. This position is best represented by Barbara Boyd's book *Ovid's Literary Loves*, which makes a compelling case for the literary complexity of the *Amores*.[32] Boyd explicates the literary ambition of the *Amores*, by demonstrating its relationship with epic (among other literary traditions),[33] and by offering a sustained set of reflections on the dynamics of imitation, intertextuality and allusion, which anticipate some of the probing analyses of these devices that Stephen Hinds would offer in *Allusion and Intertext*, published the following year.[34] This approach seeks to wrest Ovid away from the position in which he is commonly cast as narrow elegiac imitator in order to parse the *Amores* as a far richer literary construction. Yet for all her attempts to eschew the structures of thought responsible for dismissing the *Amores* as parody, Boyd does retain one of the most persistent of these, which is the separation of the poet-lover, as the first person *ego* of love elegy is commonly identified, into two separate entities.[35] The effect of this separation is made clear by the chapter title in which Boyd articulates it, 'From Authenticity to Irony':[36] where the coherence of the poet-lover as a singular entity was a mark of the authenticity of the poetry he wrote in the name of desire, the separation of these two aspects of his persona becomes a source of ironic commentary. It is precisely

---

32   Boyd 1997.

33   Cf. esp. Boyd 1997, 49–89 (Chapter 2 'Literary Means and Ends: Ovid's *Ludus Poeticus*'), which focuses on Ovid's use of Vergil as a window onto prior literary history; and 90–131 (Chapter 3: 'Ovid's Visual Memory: Extended Similes in the *Amores*'), which bases its discussion on what this device owes to epic.

34   Hinds 1998 is discussed in greater detail in my section on the *Metamorphoses* on pp. 25–27 below.

35   Bretzigheimer 2001, 11–46 offers one of the most sustained attempts to close the gap between the poet/lover, by reading the *Amores* as an elaborate exercise in metapoetics, one that makes poetry itself the object of the erotic discourse that the collection stages. Holzberg 1997, 55–74, by contrast, like others before him, maintains a degree of separation between the two components of the *poeta/amator* hybrid, and points to places where they operate in tension with one another.

36   Boyd 1997, 132–164.

this separation that earlier critics used to justify the *Amores'* status as parody, and Boyd's description of the effect as irony does seem like something of a concession to this view.

Both Kennedy and Boyd substantially advance the scholarship on the *Amores* beyond earlier discussions that had dismissed this work as 'mere' parody. Yet in many ways they do so by demonstrating that the parodic effect that earlier critics had noticed is an effect of the discursive status of erotic poetry, a status that Ovid's predecessors may have sought to occlude, but about which Ovid himself is simply transparent. In exploding the fictions of authenticity that had attached to ideas of the poet-lover in the name of discourse, these scholars explicate a feature that Frederic Jameson presents as a hallmark of post-modernism, which is what he describes as the 'waning of affect.'[37] With this phrase, Jameson conjures the flatness or depthlessness of the post-modern aesthetic, represented in this essay by Andy Warhol's *Diamond Dust Shoes*, and the lack of emotion that such images inspire because of their detachment from a relatable life or life-world.[38] Jameson explicates the deathly quality of the Warhol image by noting what it owes to the photographic negative: its 'glaced X-ray elegance mortifies the reified eye of the viewer in a way that would seem to have nothing to do with death or the death obsession or the death anxiety on the level of content,' but which marks 'some more fundamental mutation both in the object world itself – now become a set of texts or simulacra – and in the disposition of the subject.'[39] The distinction that Jameson draws here between Warhol's image and a classic work of high modernism by Van Gogh, along with the implicit critique of the post-modern aesthetic, maps onto certain differences we might note between the aesthetic prerogatives of Ovid and Propertius, and the critical distaste that the former has inspired in certain critics compared with the latter. The depthlessness, the lack of a relatable life world (because it is so transparently not there), its status as pure text or *simulacrum*, are all things we could say about Ovid's *Amores*. In addition, there is the compensation that Jameson finds in *Diamond Dust Shoes* for its absenting of affect: the decorative exhilaration it displays in the sheen of glittering gold dust on the surface of the image.[40] This too is there in

---

37 Jameson 1991, 6–16 (p. 10 for the phrase).

38 Jameson's point of comparison is Van Gogh's painting of the boots of a peasant ('*A Pair of Shoes*'), a work of high modernism in which the work of art serves to mediate between the painted object and the life-world that viewers are invited to imagine for it. Cf. Jameson 1991, 6–8 for discussion.

39 Jameson 1991, 9.

40 Jameson 1991, 10.

the *Amores*, in the sheer ebullience of the poet's (or poet-lover's) transparently discursive performances.

Jameson's critique of Warhol's aesthetic is primarily ideological, premised on this artist's depoliticised engagement with consumer culture: 'The great billboard images of the Coca-Cola bottle or the Campbell's soup can, which explicitly foreground the commodity fetishism of a transition to late capital, *ought* to be powerful and critical political statements.' If they are not, it may be because these works have a more subtle point to make about the relationship between consumerism and desire than Jameson is prepared to allow, their depthless aesthetic and habit of substituting the *simulacrum* for the object itself a comment on the absences that drive desire in an economy mobilised by the spectre of capital and by the fantasies delivered by mass advertising. This opens up another avenue for thinking about Ovid's *Amores*, one that has done more to close the parodic (or ironic) gap between poetry and its object in this collection than any other critical approach in recent times. Whatever it means to say that the *Amores* is 'about' love, it is certainly about desire, and presents to readers a performance of desire in action that responds well to twentieth century psychoanalytical readings. Philip Hardie was among the first to recuperate this aspect of Ovid's writing in recent times in his study of Ovidian illusionism, which places desire at the centre of this poetic technique.[41] As Hardie points out, desire is founded on absence – the object of desire is always absent to a greater or lesser degree. According to this view, the absences at the heart of the *Amores*, far from expressing the poet's depthlessness, carry important insights into the nature and dynamics of desire.[42]

The name of the elegiac *puella* provides Hardie with his starting point for considering the absences at the heart of language itself, as he reminds us how the name that should make the erotic object most present serves more often than not to remind us of the multiple ways in which s/he is in fact absent. This may be true of all proper names (which are all, more or less, detachable), but it is doubly true of the pseudonyms of erotic elegy, where names such as Cynthia, Delia, and Corinna inscribe a set of male fantasies that are transparently literary fictions. And it is the transparently textual status of the erotic object in the

---

41   Hardie 2002a, 11: "Desire may well be the master-term for an understanding of Ovid's poetics of illusion, and a mildly polemical aim of this book is to reclaim Ovid as one of the great writers of desire in the western tradition."

42   Hardie 2002a, 31: "... I suggest that two features of Ovid's love poetry often viewed as indices of an underlying lack of seriousness or commitment, firstly the emptiness and unreality of the Ovidian erotic object, and secondly the writtenness of Ovidian scenes and narratives of desire, so far from being the symptoms of frivolity and detachment, are rather signs of a searching engagement with the structures and dynamics of desire."

Amores that provides Hardie with much of the basis for his Lacanian approach to desire in this work. For Lacan, the individual subject (often referred to as the barred subject because of the way in which the symbolic alienates subjects from themselves, even as it constitutes them) is formed in (and/or mediated by) the realm of the symbolic, which is the domain of language, culture, and social codes, into which she is thrown at birth.[43] These pre-given codes and contexts structure the subject (including her unconscious) like a language, yet the desire for an imagined place of wholeness that existed prior to language, and which language has displaced, persists,[44] revealing itself in the gaps that open up between need and demand. Desire arises as the surplus that exceeds the meeting of a particular need by a demand articulated in language (and hence within the symbolic), a desire to be recognised (or desired) by the Other.[45] Through a process of symbolic castration, the subject understands that the desires of the Other circulate around a Master-signifier, and seeks out signifiers through which he can approximate to it.[46] Hardie demonstrates how the elusive hunt for the erotic object through the opening sequence of the *Amores* stages this procedure for readers, above all because the textual and/or linguistic status of that object brings out the way in which Lacanian desire operates both in and for the symbolic Other. Far from seeing the transparent fiction that Corinna is as a parody of Propertius's treatment of 'Cynthia,' Hardie demonstrates how realistic this narrative of desire is, insofar as the erotic object always seems to hide behind screens and signifiers. Hardie draws on Peter Brooks' *Body Works* in order to unpack the screening effect at work in *Amores* 1.5, where the fragmentation of the beloved's body that we encounter in the anatomy of her nakedness, which should make her most transparently present, does as much to frustrate our scopophilia (and concomitant epistemophilia).[47]

While Hardie models his account of Ovidian desire in the *Amores* primarily on Lacanian theory, his mention of Peter Brooks brings up an alternative psychoanalytical model of desire, which has provided critics with another

---

43 Hardie 2002a, 31–32; with Janan 1994, 21–26.

44 Gasperoni 1996, 82: "What was lost in gaining the power of speech can never be enunciated, but this does not mean it goes away. The empty place where it is supposed once to have been remains. It insists as desire."

45 This is explicated most clearly in Lacan 2006, 575–584.

46 The subject who identifies as female develops a different relation to the phallus, as discussed on p. 21 below.

47 Hardie 2002a, 40–44, with discussion of Brooks 1992 on p. 41. See Brooks 1992, 99, for discussion of the relationship between the Freudian instincts of scopophilia (the desire to see someone's genitals) and epistemophilia (the desire for knowledge).

powerful toolset for analysing the libidinal economy of this text. Ellen Oliensis'
recent book on the *Amores* is a tour de force of Freudian criticism, one that
builds on her earlier application of Freudian analysis to a wider range of
Latin poets,[48] but which here zeros in on Freud's various theories of sexuality, and uses these insights to scrutinize the erotic stratagems and dynamics
seen in this particular work of erotic elegy.[49] A key text for Oliensis is Freud's
Three Essays on Sexuality, which sets out (in its opening essay) to debunk the
assumption that our sexual drives arrive 'bundled with a particular object (heterosexual, adult, human) and aim (gratification via genital intercourse).'[50] In
fact, as Oliensis glosses, Freud insists that divergence from this expected sexual
path is perfectly normal, and frequently wanders into (and onto) areas other
than the genital zone, and away from sexual intercourse into other 'subordinate' sexual activities (e.g. touching and looking). She draws on this insight
in order to track the sexual 'waywardness' that the *Amores* stages: on the
strange fact, for example, that the *Amores* has both a singular erotic object (in
the form of Corinna) and multiple others at the same time;[51] on the protagonist's greater addiction to the torturous frustration of desire than to its plea-
surable gratification;[52] on his preoccupation with literal (as well as figurative)
castration,[53] the destruction of paternal authority,[54] and with sexual fantasies
about mothers and ideas of maternity;[55] and on the capacity for 'writing poetry'
to operate as one of those subordinate sexual activities (such as touching and
looking) that may come to substitute for sexual intercourse itself.[56] With this

---

48   Oliensis 2009.

49   Oliensis 2019.

50   Oliensis 2019, 105–106 (quotation on 105).

51   Oliensis 2019, 106–110.

52   Oliensis 2019, 110–127, with discussion of how the exquisitely painful pleasure of frustra-
      tion, documented throughout the *Amores*, relates to the psychosexual pleasures of mas-
      ochism (as similarly displayed in the novel by Sacher-Masoch *Venus in Furs*) from p. 112.

53   Oliensis 2019, 127–130 notes the resemblance between the literally castrated eunuch,
      Bagoas, of *Am.* 2.2 and 2.3 and the figuratively castrated, or in this instance 'locked out',
      lover.

54   Oliensis 2019, 130–136 notes the patent subversion of father figures – be they literal, liter-
      ary (e.g. Vergil), or cultural (e.g. Augustus) – throughout the *Amores*, most especially in
      Ovid's habit of ventriloquizing the paternal perspective within this inappropriate con-
      text. See esp. her compelling reading on pp. 134–135 of how Ovid misapplies the tools of
      his education by (for example) applying his mathematical skills to counting the metrical
      feet of elegiac poetry.

55   Oliensis 2019, 136–149 focuses on the maternal fantasies visible in the two abortion poems
      (*Am.* 2.13 and 2.14), but ranges beyond these to note how these fantasies spill into sur-
      rounding poems in book 2, esp. *Am.* 2.15, the ring poem.

56   Oliensis 2019, 150–188.

final theme, Oliensis finds a way of overcoming that split between poetry and love, which haunts earlier criticism of the *Amores*, by making poetry not the medium of desire but its object. Oliensis' Freudian model not only provides a brilliant (and hilarious) framework for unpacking many of the absurdities, and seemingly absurd truths, of Ovidian erotics, but, along with Hardie's Lacanian model (and in complementary terms to his), a means of fusing the medium of Ovid's poetry with its content.

However, in the course of explicating her vision and version of the poet-lover of the *Amores*,[57] Oliensis runs up against an aspect of this text that will prove to be problematic (and especially so) for the reception of the *Ars Amatoria* in the twenty-first century as well. As she points out, 'Naso hardly seems like a plausible vehicle for any self-respecting human being's desire. Naso is an abominable character.'[58] If this is true of Naso, the protagonist of the *Amores*, it is doubly true of Naso, the *magister amoris* of the *Ars Amatoria*, who so detaches himself from the narrative of elegiac *amor* that he can teach its abominable ploys as a system. For some critics, this is (paradoxically) why the *Ars Amatoria* may be read as conforming with Augustan civic ideals: *amor* is as culturally coded as any other social institution in Rome, and may be organised and taught in the same way as the *officia* of Cicero's *de Officiis*.[59] The fact that this system presents itself as an amusing literary game does little to exonerate this text of the charges of exploitation and male violence on which its didactic message is premised. Oliensis notes the various ways in which certain scholars have attempted to negotiate this aspect of the *Amores*, and provide the poet with a redemptive alibi for his abominable creation: by arguing, for example, that the very depravity of the poet-lover's behaviour, and the poet's apparent detachment from this persona, carry a latent moral critique of the effects of *amor*, and of the chauvinist assumptions on which elegy's codes are premised.[60] This too is a line that one could take to the *Ars Amatoria*: its endorsement of rape as a permissible action can be taken as a *reductio ad absurdum* of love

---

57 Oliensis 2019, 14–19 adopts the strategy (maintained throughout the rest of the book) of calling the poet-lover Naso, in order to make clear the distinction between this fictional persona and the Ovidian author, while maintaining the coherence of the poet-lover as a singular entity (rather than splitting him into 'poet' and 'lover' as many earlier critics do).

58 Oliensis 2019, 102. See also p. 10 n. 11 for her brusque appraisal of Mick Jagger.

59 Labate 1984, 121–174 draws extensive parallels between the *Ars* and Cic. *Off.* in the context of a study that seeks to recuperate the educational project of the *Ars Amatoria* by demonstrating the affinities between the protocols and customs of lovers and those of other social relationships in Rome. Myerowitz 1985 offers an alternative view of the cultural project that the *Ars* seeks to encode, by emphasising its attempt to impose order and convention on an emotion (*amor*) that is inherently disorderly and unpredictable.

60 Cf. e.g. Cahoon 1988, 294; Greene 1998, 113; and James 2003, 198.

elegy's logic, an exposure of the problematic conflict between ends and means that the other elegists seldom (if ever) address. But this argument ignores the objection that many modern readers raise as to why this literary game has to play out at the expense of a woman's body. We are taught to think of this as an anachronistic objection, yet as Amy Richlin has shown, this is only because we are conditioned to assume that the only valid (or indeed possible) lens onto ancient Rome is the male one.[61] In ignoring the perspective of the female in a text like this, we fall into the danger of appearing to endorse the text's surface messages in contexts where they are liable to be misconstrued.[62] We also fail to answer how this text responds to women's desires, both then and now. Given that Ovid himself directly addresses a female readership in the *Ars Amatoria*, why have critics historically been so reluctant to consider how it answers to female interests?[63]

These two objections are ones that we could likewise raise for the *Amores*, and bring with them a correlated set of objections to Oliensis' approach to this text, objections that relate directly to her Freudian model. Freud's theories of sexuality are notoriously male-oriented, and have inspired many a feminist critique: his theories of castration anxiety and penis envy, for example, are premised on the central importance of the male penis, to the extent that the female is defined, for this drive at least, by her lack.[64] Any reading of desire in the *Amores*, or the *Ars Amatoria*, that is premised on Freud's *Theories of Sexuality* cannot help but reinforce a male perspective on these texts, one that their protagonists already seem to invite, however much Oliensis' Freudian emphasis on the waywardness of the sexual drives swerves away from sexual consummation, violent or otherwise.[65] What can a reading of the *Amores* that is premised on Freud's *Theories of Sexuality* do to address the interests or desires of twenty-first century women – homosexual, heterosexual, bisexual, bicurious

---

61 Richlin 2014, 1–35.

62 Zuckerberg 2018 details the sanction that modern pick-up artists have sought in the *Ars Amatoria*.

63 The major exception to this rule is Rimell 2006, 70–103 (discussed on pp. 17–18 below).

64 The partial corrective that Lacanian psychoanalysis provides to this view, wherein the Phallus has a purely structural function, one that operates for both sexes, and has less to do with biology than with its place in the Symbolic, may be one of the reasons why some Latinists have felt more comfortable reading texts through its lens. But see Rimell 2019, 8 n. 31, for a summary of literature detailing feminist objections to the predication of Lacanian desire on the Phallus.

65 Martelli 2013, 68–103 offers an alternative Freudian model of reading one of Ovid's erotic works (the *Ars Amatoria*), by viewing the erotic 'plot' of the *Ars* through the lens of Freud's *Beyond the Pleasure Principle*, a work of Freud's that does not present the same pitfalls for questions of gender as his *Theories of Sexuality*, even if it doubtless opens up others.

or otherwise? Female readers are, of course, at liberty to identify with the desires of the male protagonists of these poems if they wish to. In her critique of the fantasies of violence against women that many of Ovid's texts appear to project, Richlin draws on the theory of fantasy developed by Laplanche and Pontalis, wherein the subject can oscillate between multiple positions.[66] With fantasies of sexual violence, the reader may identify either with the rapist (and experience a vicarious sadistic pleasure), or with the victim (and experience a vicarious masochistic thrill), alternative subject positions that are both available for female as well as male readers to take up. Yet as Richlin points out, this does not constitute an escape from a system of thought in which sexual violence is inscribed into the unequal power relations that sustain it in the name of gender – even when that violence is forestalled.

One recent work of scholarship that proffers a promising route out of this impasse is Victoria Rimell's book, *Ovid's Lovers*, which addresses the topic of intersubjectivity across Ovid's oeuvre, including within and between *Ars* 1–2 (which is notionally addressed to men) and *Ars* 3 (addressed to women).[67] As Rimell suggests, this neat separating out of discretely gendered groups of readers between the two units is deconstructed by the fact that *Ars* 1–2 may 'nudge an imaginary female readership to read between the lines,' while *Ars* 3 includes asides for the benefit of male readers.[68] According to Rimell, the three book *Ars* not only includes the perspectives of both men and women, but also sets them at cross-purposes, as the *magister* deliberately undermines his own advice to each group by letting the other one in on his secrets, an argument that radically challenges the idea that the female in this text is only ever the object of male sexual fantasy. Rimell draws on the paradigm of Medusa as a model for the castrating effects of the empowered female gaze, and points up the places where we find this model aligned with the female love 'object' in the *Ars Amatoria*, in an attempt to recuperate a subject position for her within it.[69] She also highlights the numerous places in this text where the story of Narcissus resonates – in the amoebean echoes of the elegiac couplet, for

---

66   Richlin 2014, 159.

67   Where other scholars prior to Rimell had discussed the address to women in *Ars* 3, their readings underscore the unequal power relations that this book appears to set up with their male counterparts in *Ars* 1–2: both Myerowitz 1985 and Downing 1990 view women as passive objects, either of active (male) erotic conquest, or of elegiac construction.

68   Rimell 2006, 74. Miller 1994, 238–241 and Gibson 2003, 19–21 note the asides to male readers in *Ars* 3. But without noting the implied presence of a female readership in *Ars* 1–2, their readings contribute to the prevailing view of unequal power relations in the *Ars* that Rimell is at pains to rebuff.

69   Rimell 2006 draws on the way in which French feminists, such as Irigaray and Cixous, reframe the argument of Freud 1922 for the perspective of the woman.

example – both within the discrete units of *Ars* 1–2 and 3, and across them. Men and women are made to resemble one another in this text, such that we can never finally say who has the upper hand in its narratives of erotic manipulation.[70] Her chapter closes with a reading of the Procris and Cephalus episode from *Ars* 3, which argues that neither character is as innocent as they seem, and thereby presents a mise-en-abyme of the gendered dynamics scripted throughout the entire work.[71]

Rimell's study of intersubjectivity ranges beyond the *Ars Amatoria* to take in a range of other Ovidian texts, with particular mileage gained from the *Heroides*, in which male and female voices and perspectives coexist either through ventriloquism (in the single epistles, *Heroides* 1–15) or juxtaposition (in the paired letters, *Heroides* 16–20). In the case of the *Heroides*, intersubjectivity is a particular inflection of the feminist discourses that started flooding these texts in the early 2000s, when gender replaced intertextuality as the dominant critical term for their analysis.[72] The emphasis on the intertextual fabric of the *Heroides*, which had earlier held sway, privileged the male author, Ovid, and the games that he was playing with a (predominantly) male literary canon over the heads of the female heroines who appeared to give unwitting voice to these complex literary interactions. Foundational to this approach was Kennedy's 1984 reading of *Heroides* 1, in which he demonstrated that Ovid's voicing of Penelope in the fictional epistle he composes for her is cut through with certain ironies, because it intervenes in the master narrative of the *Odyssey* at a quite particular point: namely, when Odysseus has come to the palace disguised as a beggar. When Penelope reveals that she is writing the letter with the intention of handing it to this stranger to carry overseas in the hope of finding her absent husband, the reader familiar with the master narrative enjoys the irony of knowing, as she does not, that she will be delivering the letter directly to its intended addressee. This approach was subsequently developed by a group of scholars in Italy, who set out to reveal a similar set of ironies in the other epistles all at the heroines' expense.[73] Barchiesi, one of the most sensitive and prolific readers of the *Heroides*' intertextual complexity and a critic who anticipated the ensuing feminist wave of scholarship on the poems to some extent,[74] famously described the heroines of the *Heroides* as,

---

70   Rimell 2006, 76–83.
71   Rimell 2006, 94–103.
72   E.g. Spentzou 2003; Lindheim 2003; and Fulkerson 2005.
73   Cf. esp. Casali 1995a and 1995b.
74   Cf. e.g. Barchiesi 1995, 327. Rosati 1992 also offers a corrective to the prevailing focus on the male perspective of the 'master narratives' by tracing the way in which the heroines construct an elegiac *ego* for themselves. Bessone 1997 likewise makes a forceful case for

'vittime e prigioniere di troppa letteratura' ('victims and prisoners of too much literature').[75] A quick succession of books on the collection, informed by various aspects of feminist theory, set out to release Ovid's female captives, and their voices, from this male prison-house of literature.

This endeavour began in earnest with the publication in 2003 of Efrossini Spentzou's *Readers and Writers in Ovid's Heroides*, a work that explicitly countered the predominant mode of understanding intertextuality in Classics by taking it back to its Kristevan foundations. Kristeva coined the term intertextuality in a series of studies on the work of Mikhael Bakhtin, whose ideas of polyphony, dialogism and heteroglossia inform her understanding of the term.[76] Her view of intertextuality as dialogic has a role to play in her vision of language more generally, which contests the Saussurean view of a closed, predictable system, and which rather makes space for the disruptive effects of the speaking subject. For Kristeva, signification (of which language is an example) does not follow a universal law, but is frequently overtaken by signifying processes determined by the drives and by semiotic operations that are anterior to language.[77] Signification consists of the interactions between these latter operations (which Kristeva dubs the semiotic) and the symbolic (which conforms, more or less, to the Lacanian register of the same name). The subject who speaks is a 'subject in process' – that is, a subject constituted and reconstituted by the processes of signification (and the semiotic and symbolic registers that intersect it) that are channelled through her.[78] Spentzou enlists Kristeva's idea of the speaking subject for her own interpretation of how Ovid's heroines disrupt the literary system in which their narratives have hitherto been framed, and attempts to recuperate the various ways in which the women resist their master narratives, by giving voice to all that those narratives repress.[79]

Drawing in particular on the use that Kristeva makes of the Platonic *chora*, an inert, feminine space in which the prelinguistic pulses of the semiotic order are gathered,[80] Spentzou suggests that this offers an apt way of thinking about the place from which the heroines speak, and about the discourse that

---

a gendered rewriting of the canon in her study of *Her.* 12 (Medea to Jason), in which, she argues, Medea anticipates her (past) literary futures (in the Euripidean and even Ovidian tragedies that bear her name) not as victim but as conspiratorial planner.

75   Barchiesi 1994, 112.
76   Cf. esp. Kristeva 1981, 64–91, 'Word, Dialogue, and Novel'.
77   Kristeva 1984, 25–31.
78   Kristeva 1984, 101.
79   Cf. esp. Spentzou 2003, 22–33.
80   Kristeva 1984, 25–31.

emanates from such a place.[81] The domestic domain within which Penelope weaves and unweaves Laertes' shroud is presented as an exemplary analogue of the Kristevan *chora*: a feminine enclosure within which time is suspended, and where the symbolic (male) order represented by the shroud is subjected to a repeated and repetitious process of unpicking as a means of resisting narrative closure.[82] This model presents an avenue for recuperating many of the features (e.g. repetition) that have most embarrassed scholarship on the *Heroides* in the name of the feminine. Spentzou also draws on Cixous' vision of *l'écriture féminine* in order to draw out the qualities of the heroines' discursive resistance.[83] The 'carnal alphabet' of the heroines' emanations, wherein verbal messages are (apparently) blotted with blood and tears;[84] metonymical displacement, which allows thought to wander across contiguous relationships;[85] and the free association of metaphorical play are some of the characteristics of their epistles that Spentzou picks out as examples of the Ovidian heroines' distinctively feminine writing.[86]

Sara Lindheim's book on the *Heroides*, published in the same year as Spentzou's, is ostensibly written on similar premises, insofar as she too turns her attention toward the significance of the heroines' gender for the collection.[87] But because her reading takes closer account of the male author behind the heroines' writing, it draws on a different set of theoretical tools and reaches a very different set of conclusions to Spentzou's. Lindheim's study is particularly sensitive to the epistolary status of these texts, and to the way in which gender, or, more particularly, gendered desire, is configured by the structure of the epistle. As she notes, while the authors of the letters are ostensibly female (or 'female'), their addressees are all male: these texts address themselves to a male readership, and configure their stories around their male addressees, who, as objects of the heroines' desire, remain the true protagonists. Rather than using the opportunity afforded by the letter to write their own subjectivity into the centre of the stories in which they feature, the heroines' fixation on the absence of their male lovers serves instead to re-emphasise

---

81   Spentzou 2003, 103: "it is a discourse that disrupts and disputes the Symbolic accounts of the forefathers of the classical narratives, marking their absences, contradicting their complacent certainties and occasionally keeping a silence that can muffle the clamour of boisterous epic and tragedy."

82   Spentzou 2003, 103–104.

83   Spentzou 2003, 110 on Cixous and Clement 1986, 96.

84   Spentzou 2003, 105–111.

85   Spentzou 2003, 116–118.

86   Spentzou 2003, 117–121 on the features of Cixous' conception of *écriture féminine*.

87   Lindheim 2003.

their marginal status within these stories.[88] The most characteristic features of the epistolary medium – namely, its capacity to conjure the illusion of the addressee's presence as interlocutor by seeming to transcend the spatial (and temporal) distance between them in anticipation of a response – is patently exploded by these letters, which receive no replies, and which, in many cases, are written without the expectation of being delivered (or even sent). The medium is thus made to work against them, as Ovid uses the epistle to promote the view offered by Sophocles' *Trachiniae* (the source text for *Heroides* 9) that the female (in this case Deianira) is a writing tablet, 'a passive medium for male writing and reading,' in this case for the writing of male fantasy.[89]

Lindheim proceeds to show how Ovid's heroines construct themselves in ways that conform with Lacan's account of feminine desire. According to Lacan, the female subject differs from the male with respect to the experience of castration that every subject undergoes when they encounter the symbolic loss of the Phallus – that is, the realization that the mother's desire lies elsewhere. While the male subject responds to this experience by seeking out fragments of the Phallus (in the form of *objets a*) in anticipation of becoming the bearer of an object that would satisfy a lover, the female seeks not to possess the Phallus (or its fragments) but to attract someone who appears to have it.[90] Lindheim posits this Lacanian view of feminine desire as a model for considering the various roles that the individual heroines play in these epistles in their attempt to make themselves answer to the desire of the Other (who is, in this case, the male addressee).[91] But Lindheim notes the limitations placed on the variety of roles available to Ovid's heroines, and argues finally that the iterative quality of the *Heroides*, and the heroines' resemblance to one another, makes this collection amount to a male fantasy about Woman: that is, it presents a generalizing attempt to construct Woman out of women, in precisely the way that Lacan suggests is impossible.[92] This conclusion emerges with particular clarity in her discussion of *Heroides* 15, Sappho's letter to Phaon, where the stereotypical heroine that Ovid presents to readers is clearly at odds with the authoress with whom readers are familiar, whose subjectivity appears from her poetry as heterogeneous, fragmentary, or, in Lacanian terms, not-whole.[93]

---

88   Cf. esp. Lindheim 2003, 30–77.

89   Lindheim 2003, 65.

90   Lacan 1998.

91   Lindheim 1998, 89–135. Cf. esp. her reading (at pp. 114–134) of how Hypsipyle and Medea (rivals for Jason's love) construct themselves in the mirror-image of each other in *Heroides* 6 and 12.

92   Lindheim 2003, 133–135 on Lacan's assertions about Woman at Lacan 1998, 72–73.

93   Lindheim 2003, 136–176.

Lindheim and Spentzou present us with a critical diptych on the *Heroides*: a pair of readings that take quite different views of the female prisoners within these texts, predicated in each case on different theoretical grounds, the one informed by French feminism, the other by Lacanian psychoanalysis. Again, Rimell points a way out of the impasse, insofar as her focus on intersubjectivity in the double *Heroides* as well as in *Heroides* 15 opens up a space for two competing gendered perspectives.[94] Rimell's reading of the coincidence of Ovidian and Sapphic voices in *Heroides* 15, for example, presents a more densely woven picture of male and female intersubjectivity than Lindheim allows. The voice of the female poetess irrupts through Ovidian elegy, in the unusually graphic expression of erotic desire and in the homoerotic hints that coexist alongside her desire for Phaon,[95] even as Ovid's own voice moves to silence her.[96] This produces a competition of genders and authorial hands: the lyric poet turned elegist writes mournful poetry about unrequited love and laments the loss of inspiration that comes with this state, as if to assert the superiority of her previous lyric compositions. When she reminds the reader that her fame (*qua* poetess) already spreads across the world, this might look like another assertion of the superiority of Sapphic lyric to Ovidian elegy; but as Rimell points out, it is phrased in terms that remind us unmistakably of similar assertions that Ovid makes about his own fame in his other amatory works, such that it becomes again impossible to know which authorial voice to choose from here.[97] Rimell deftly demonstrates that the questions of authenticity that have long overshadowed *Heroides* 15 may well derive from the complexity of its artful experiment in authorial intersubjectivity.[98]

Scholarship on Ovid's amatory works has now arrived at a point that insists on acknowledging the desires, interests, and subjectivities of the female.

---

94   A major pay-off of Rimell 2006, is that its central theme of intersubjectivity provides a compelling framework for appraising *Heroides* 16–21 (the 'double *Heroides*') as a collection. Prior to her reading of the paired epistles (on pp. 156–179), very few scholars (with the exception of e.g. Hintermeier 1993; Kenney 1996; and Barchiesi 1999) had treated *Her.* 16–21 in detail as a collection.

95   Rimell 2006, 136–137 on the significance of Sappho's 'lubricious' account of her wet dream at *Her.* 15.133–134, and on the rewriting of *Am.* 1.5 as 'lesbian erotica' with the description at *Her.* 15. 161–162 of the sensual apparition of a Naiad.

96   Rimell 2006, 137–138 notes the reminiscence of the aposiopesis in *Am.* 1.5.23–26 at *Her.* 15.133.

97   Rimell 2006, 147 on *Her.* 15.28, which echoes the confident predictions of fame at *Am.* 1.3.26 and also *Am.* 1.15.7–8.

98   Rimell 2006, 152–154 relates her argument about the letter's intersubjective relations to the question of its authenticity. Tarrant 1981; Murgia 1985; and Knox 1995, 12–14, have all argued that *Heroides* 15 is not written by Ovid but by an Ovidian imitator.

Whether by concentrating on how Ovid parodies the chauvinistic premises of erotic elegy's discourse in the *Amores*, or by considering how an acknowledged female readership in the *Ars Amatoria* complicates the ostensible didactic goals of this text, or by unpacking the layers of gender at work in Ovid's attempts to ventriloquise the voices of female heroines in the *Heroides*: the critical momentum in scholarship on all of Ovid's erotic works lies squarely with those scholars who have developed approaches to these texts that explicitly proffer a route into them for the female. It is no doubt a sign of the times that one of the most recent works of scholarship to treat Ovid's early amatory works *in toto* considers the entirety of this *corpus* through the lens of *Heroides* 15. Thea Thorsen's study of this corpus focuses on the dense network of allusions to the *Amores*, *Ars Amatoria*, and the rest of the single *Heroides* that are contained within this epistle in order to argue the case for seeing this text as mise-en-abyme of the entirety of Ovid's erotic *corpus*, and for viewing its portrait of Sappho, the authoress, as a fitting reflection of the Ovidian *auctor*.[99] Long dismissed as inauthentic,[100] and deemed unworthy of critical attention, *Heroides* 15 has now moved to the centre of scholarly discourse on Ovid's erotic works, its complex negotiation of gendered authorship a fitting platform for authorizing the female interests that have come to attach to these works in our own time. While certain waves of feminism share affiliations with post-structuralism, their common focus on female interests and perspectives transcends that critical movement, which may help explain why feminist approaches to these texts remain in the ascendant.

3   *Metamorphoses* (i): Between Nature and Culture

Of all the texts that can be said to have benefited from the new critical idiom that began to infiltrate Ovidian scholarship over three decades ago, the *Metamorphoses* stands out for the range of different ways in which its aesthetic and philosophical prerogatives answer to the demands of that critical turn. Ovid's interest in the absences that drive desire remains a prominent narrative theme in this text, while his skill at making abstractions materialise at the surface of language is also demonstrably on show. The self-consciousness with which he riffs on the preceding literary tradition remains familiar from

---

99   Thorsen 2014.
100   Cf. esp. Tarrant 1981. Thorsen 2014, 96–122 offers an extensive survey of scholarship on the presumed inauthenticity of *Heroides* 15, including a discussion (and critique) of the premises of Tarrant's influential arguments.

his earlier works, but takes on a more expansive scope within the capacious parameters of epic. Scholarship on the *Metamorphoses* adds to these familiar topics of Ovidian criticism a further interest in the crossing of genres, and in the contingencies of narrative situation and context, as the majority of the stories recounted within the *Metamorphoses* are placed in the hands (or voices) of its numerous internal narrators. If a defining characteristic of post-modernism is its manner of eschewing grand narratives, then the narratological complexity of the *Metamorphoses* proffers one means by which Ovid tempers the traditional linearity of epic's narrative form, while the poem's generic hybridity deflates the tonal grandiosity associated with epic as a genre. Ovid's poem traces a broad narrative arc from rough, uncultivated nature to civilised culture, although the two remain mutually entwined throughout, as we shall see. In this section, I will survey some of the highlights of the past thirty years of scholarship on the *Metamorphoses*, conducted under the broad influence of post-structuralism, which has arguably done more to elucidate those aspects of the poem's cultivated veneer (its form and style) than it has done for its thematic content. I will then set out at greater length a new approach to the poem, one that takes particular account of the relationship between nature and culture that it traces, which I believe will be another significant direction for scholarship on the poem in the years to come.

The new era of scholarship on the *Metamorphoses* began (in the anglophone world, at least)[101] in 1987 with a publication that instantiated the formalist bias of much that would follow: Stephen Hinds' study of Ovid's parallel narratives of the Proserpina myth in *Metamorphoses* 5 and *Fasti* 4. This book is avowedly traditional in the questions that it asks of the poem, which focus on the generic constraints placed on Ovid's narrative techniques,[102] but novel in its approach to answering those questions – and novel too in its view of the literary sensibility it reveals in the course of answering them. In particular, Hinds demonstrates the self-consciousness with which Ovid signposts the generic parameters of each of his renderings of this narrative. For example, the reference in the *Met.* 5 story to the hardness of Pegasus' hoof, which created

---

101 Rosati 1983 is a comparably significant landmark of twentieth century scholarship on the *Metamorphoses* in the Italian-speaking world. See my discussion on p. 29 below.

102 In particular, Hinds both endorses and builds upon the approach of Heinze 1919, which similarly takes up the invitation posed by the parallel narratives of the Proserpina myth in the *Fasti* and *Metamorphoses* to compare the generic contours of Ovid's narrative technique in these two texts, and which highlights the epic features of the *Metamorphoses* version, and the elegiac features of the *Fasti* version. In broadly endorsing Heinze's conclusions, Hinds bucks a critical trend that had set in to dismiss Heinze's findings as overschematic.

the Hippocrene when it struck Mount Helicon, taps into a generic dichotomy of hard epic and soft (or light) elegy, which is sustained elsewhere in the *Fasti* by a reference (in *Fasti* 3) to the Hippocrene being created by the appropriately light (*levis*) hoof of Pegasus. And the laments that characterise the *Fasti* 4 narrative as distinctively elegiac (by alluding to elegy's origins in lament) are phrased at certain points in ways that also draw attention to the echoing, alternating form of the elegiac couplet. At stake in these readings is an attention to poetic form, not simply for its effect on the shaping of narrative content, but as a means of generating narrative in and of itself, because of the way in which the formal features of a text make that text a very precise intervention in literary history.

While the emphasis of Hinds' argument in *The Metamorphosis of Proserpina* is on questions of genre (an emphasis that he maintained in subsequent studies),[103] much of his critical approach in this book concentrates on Ovid's manner of alluding to his literary predecessors, and, in particular, on the self-consciousness of his citational techniques. The dynamics of poetic allusion subsequently became the central topic of Hinds' next book, *Allusion and Intertext*, which broadens the scope of his critical inquiry to take in a much longer history of Latin poetry, from Livius Andronicus to Valerius Flaccus, and which demonstrates that similar kinds of citational self-consciousness could be found in poets other than Ovid.[104] Nevertheless, Ovid remains the most prominent and typical exponent of the knowing techniques that Hinds is at pains to describe in this book, and his readings of the *Metamorphoses* make for some of the most memorable examples of the complex dynamics of literary allusion that he scrutinizes. In an early discussion of the modes of self-reflexive annotation that poets incorporate into their allusions to other poets, Hinds proffers the example of Echo from *Met.* 4, whose name makes her an obvious site for reflecting on the dynamics of intertextual appropriation. Hinds shows how the particular mode of intertextual annotation that her name inscribes in this episode is faithful to the sonic peculiarities of the echo: her echo of the 'vale!' that Narcissus cries to his own image in the pool as he wastes away replicates the true sound of the echo as it fades by shortening the final vowel of the second *vale*. In doing so, it also 'echoes' a half-line from *Eclogues* 3, where Phyllis' reduplicated farewell to Iollas bears a similar fading echo (*et 'longum, formose, vale, vale,' inquit, 'Iolla.'*).[105] In Hinds' hands, 'Echo'

---

103   Cf. Hinds 1992, for example.
104   Hinds 1998 opens with a discussion of the 'Alexandrian footnote' exemplified by the use of *dicuntur* in the second line of Catullus 64 as a marker of allusion.
105   Hinds 1998, 5–6.

comes to stand not simply as a signpost for *any* allusion, but for an allusion to a particular kind of amoebean refrain, and he proceeds to demonstrate what scope such exchanges provide for reflecting on the dynamics of intertextual dialogue more generally.[106]

Allusion and Intertext offers more than simply a neutral description of the intertextual filiations that connect texts to one another. In showing that these filiations are never inert, but always involve active strategies of literary historical self-positioning, it takes up a particular position in a debate between exponents of allusion, on the one hand, who argue for the possibility of uncovering the author's allusive intentions; and defenders of intertextuality, on the other, who argue that the only relevant intertexts are those that the reader brings to bear on a text.[107] Hinds himself acknowledges the critical indefensibility of attempting to access an author's intentions. But he defends the idea of authorial allusion against the more reader-determined idea of intertext, by arguing that allusion is good to think with – as a discourse, 'which enables us to conceptualize and to handle certain kinds of intertextual transaction more economically and efficiently than does any alternative' (a conclusion that is borne out in practice by the compelling force of his readings).[108] Much of the book is taken up with showing how poets actively construct their literary historical lineages for their own tendentious reasons, and Ovid's *Metamorphoses* makes a brilliant case study for this argument. In an important example of this procedure, Hinds discusses Ovid's treatment of material from the *Aeneid* in *Met.* 13–14, which (he shows) amplifies the stories of metamorphosis from the precursor text – and downplays everything else – as if to reverse the determining power of the text that happens to come first by casting the *Aeneid* itself as a proto-*Metamorphoses*.[109] But if the *Metamorphoses* presents itself as a 'tendentious remake' of the *Aeneid*, it also contains episodes that seem designed to cast the *Aeneid* itself as its precursor in this technique: in the Macareus episode of *Metamorphoses* 14, Ovid reduplicates Virgil's practice of having Aeneas pick up an invented companion of Ulysses (one who claims, in each case, to have been abandoned by Ulysses on his travels), and of using this invented

---

106   Cf. esp. Hinds 1998, 6–8 on the allusion at *Met.* 3.351–355 to the repeated hymeneal refrains at Catullus 62.39–56.

107   This debate in Classics is best exemplified by a special issue of *Materiali e Discussioni* 39 (1997), which collects papers delivered at a pair of conferences in Oxford and Seattle devoted to the critical divergence between the dynamics of allusion and intertextuality. In this volume, the case for a reader-determined intertextuality is led by Don Fowler (while the case for allusion is led by Hinds).

108   Hinds 1998, 47–50.

109   Hinds 1998, 104–122.

character to recount his 'own' experience of witnessing certain adventures from his literary past. In Virgil's hands, this episode is, as Hinds highlights, a markedly post-Homeric remake: it offers a rare opportunity for Aeneas to encounter an actual member of his literary prototype's crew, and also shows that crew member replicating the first person narrative of their meeting with the Cyclops that Odysseus had himself offered in *Odyssey* 9. In picking out this particular episode from the *Aeneid*, and replicating its intertextual dynamics so faithfully in his own narrative through the dialogue conducted between Achaimenides and Macareus,[110] Ovid casts Virgil as an important precursor in the very techniques of literary doubling and appropriation that we tend to think of as distinctively Ovidian in order to forge literary histories that point squarely at himself.

The detailed attention that Hinds paid in his scholarship of the '80s and '90s to the formal dynamics of literary history did not take place in a vacuum. It was matched by a similar set of interests displayed by his contemporaries in the U.S., and also by a generation of scholars working in Italy, above all by the students of Gianbiagio Conte in Pisa.[111] We have already noted the contributions of one of the most prominent of these scholars, Alessandro Barchiesi, to scholarship on the *Heroides*. But Barchiesi's scholarship spans the entirety of Ovid's oeuvre, including the *Metamorphoses*, where it demonstrates a close affinity with the formalist prerogatives of Hinds' work. One angle that is distinct in Barchiesi's approach to the *Metamorphoses*, however, is his interest in narratology.[112] In an important article first published in 1989, Barchiesi highlighted the significant role played by internal narrators in the poem, showing how the identity of these narrators, and the literary historical past that they bring with them, inflects the stories that they tell, and revealing the narrative ironies that emerge as a result of the identity of their internal narratees.[113] This article instantiated a significant line of approach to this important aspect of the

---

110   Hinds 1998, 112 on the dizzying ramifications of the multiple intertextual configurations in play in this episode: "Amid such appropriations and reappropriations, it becomes hard to know at any given juncture whether we are responding to a Virgilian Ovid, a Homeric Virgil, or a Homeric Ovid ... or indeed to an Ovidian Virgil, a Virgilian Homer, or an Ovidian Homer." As Hinds points out, the dialogue between texts is quite literal in this passage, taking place within a conversation between these invented companions of Odysseus.

111   The identity of these Italian scholars as a group (or 'school') is marked by the fact that a number of them cut their teeth (or confirmed their status) as new Ovidians by writing commentaries on different books of the *Heroides*: Barchiesi 1992 (*Her.* 1–3); Casali 1995c (*Her.* 9); Rosati 1996 (on *Her.* 18–19); and Bessone 1997 (on *Her.* 12).

112   Enshrined (for the uninitiated) by the theme of Barchiesi 2002.

113   Barchiesi 1989 = 2001, 49–78.

poem, one that would be taken up by other scholars and developed for their own ends.[114] But Barchiesi's interest in narratology may also be seen as foundational to his approach to intertextuality, for his mapping of the mythographical continuities and discontinuities that exist between texts can be traced to a similar interest in narrative levels, and in the ironies that open up in the gaps between narrative frames.[115] Likewise, his interest in the chronological paradoxes that emerge through intertextual dialogue (which are particularly visible in those self-conscious prequels which come after a particular text in literary history but which situate their narratives at a prior point in the story) may be traced to a related interest in narratological analysis.[116]

In the case of the *Metamorphoses*, however, any interest in the poem's chronological structure, which is endlessly complicated by the multiplicity of its internal narrators, takes on a thematic and ideological significance that goes beyond literary formalism, since time is a political preoccupation of the Augustan age, and one that Ovid's poem thematises. While Barchiesi would treat the ideological dimension of Augustan time in most detail in his study of the *Fasti*,[117] he cannot help but touch on it in the course of discussing the chronological fabric of the *Metamorphoses*, most obviously in his essay on the poem's endgames.[118] The anti-closural quality of the end of the *Metamorphoses* encodes a form of resistance to Augustus' attempt to manipulate the various calendars at Rome so that they point to himself as an end of history. Other scholars who turned their attention to the chronological structure of the poem would reach a similar conclusion, and would demonstrate in the process the systematic way in which Ovid disrupts the linear temporal scheme that he advertises for the *Metamorphoses* at the outset.[119] It becomes very difficult to say whether Ovid's resistance to the idea of Augustus as an end of history is directed at the *princeps* for political reasons or is rather part of the poet's broader philosophy of time.

If this is one area where the formalist bias of a particular critical approach to the *Metamorphoses* rubs up against ideology, it is not the only one. Another

---

114   Wheeler 1999 uses the prominent presence of internal audiences to generate an approach to the poem that is informed by theories of reader response.

115   Cf. Barchiesi 1986 = 2001, 9–28. While the *Metamorphoses* is not the focus of Barchiesi's readings in this piece, it forms part of the narrative landscape that he describes.

116   This interest, exemplified in Barchiesi 1993 = 2001, 105–128, is best demonstrated by his work on the *Heroides*.

117   Barchiesi 1994b = 1997a.

118   Barchiesi 1997b.

119   Cf. Feeney 1999; Gildenhard and Zissos 1999; and Wheeler 2000 for discussion of the various games with chronology that Ovid plays in the course of the *Metamorphoses*.

significant critical line that has developed in the past thirty years focuses on the modes of visual and verbal illusionism that Ovid conjures in order to make metamorphosis materialise in ways that readers can credit. These methods have been compellingly linked to the modes of ideological make-believe current in Augustan Rome at the time of Ovid's writing. The approach began with a highly influential study by Gianpiero Rosati of Ovid's distinctive handling in the *Metamorphoses* of the myths of Narcissus and Pygmalion, which establishes the common thematic emphases of these two episodes as central to the poem's broader interest in the illusory power of vision, spectacle, and appearances, and in the illusionistic potential of language for describing these phenomena.[120] Rosati argued that the central theme of the Narcissus episode is not self-love *per se*, but illusion, and demonstrated how, in weaving together the stories of Echo and Narcissus, Ovid offers a sustained meditation on the illusory effect of visual and aural reflections. But Ovid's handling of the episode makes it offer more than a narrative description of the effects of these different types of illusion. Rather, the verbal echoes through which he conveys their effects make its theme materialise in the surface of its language, such that his narrative offers 'un caso esemplare di forma che si adegua al contenuto fino al punto di identificarsi con esso, fino a "farsi" contenuto' ('an exemplary case of form that adapts itself to content to the point of becoming identical with it, even "becoming" that content').[121] A mimetic realisation of the illusionistic nature of *imagines* so complete that the text itself stands for the reader as an analogue of the pool for Narcissus: an illusionistic lure, inviting us to believe in the reality of the appearances that it conjures.[122] Rosati points up the significance of this performance for the aesthetic principles governing the *Metamorphoses* as a whole, in part by demonstrating its continuities with the Pygmalion episode, which likewise plays with the illusionistic possibilities of mimesis (albeit by a procedure that explodes the mimetic constraints that Narcissus comes up against, in that Pygmalion's statue does come to life), and which, in casting the mythological figure of Pygmalion as an artist, makes its point specifically in relation to mimetic art. Rosati shows in detail how Ovid's illusionistic artistry plays out across the entirety of the *Metamorphoses*, alongside an allied feature of Ovidian style – namely the ekphrastic quality of his visual descriptions of metamorphosis, or, as Rosati dubs it, 'spettacolarità'.

---

120   Rosati 1983.

121   Rosati 1983, 36.

122   This reading is invited by the narrator's apostrophe to Narcissus at *Met.* 3.432–436, the implications of which are discussed at Rosati 1983, 41–46. For further discussion of the implications of this moment, see also Hardie 2002a, 147–148.

Another important study in this vein, by Garth Tissol, focuses specifically on the contribution that verbal play makes to the metamorphic texture of Ovid's language and to the experience of metamorphosis that readers derive from this text as a result.[123] Responding to a history of criticism that had dismissed as 'mere wit' the verbal games that Ovid plays through such devices as puns, aetiologies and syllepses,[124] Tissol set out to recuperate these very features as integral to a style of writing that is capable of conjuring metamorphosis in the very surface of language. Tissol managed to show that puns and word-play are seldom ornamental features of Ovid's narrative, but contribute to the stories that make up the *Metamorphoses* at the level of both theme and plot: when Echo repeats Narcissus' imperative '*coeamus*,' and imbues the verb with a sexual innuendo that Narcissus never intended, the pun contributes directly to the major theme of this episode, which addresses the illusory nature of reflections (both auditory as well as visual).[125] But when Procris misconstrues Cephalus' passionate desire for a breeze (*aura*) as an adulterous summons to a nymph named Aura, the semantic error has consequences at the level of plot when her jealousy leads her to follow Cephalus out hunting to spy on him, and he kills her mistaking her for a wild animal.[126]

As the example of Echo's *coeamus* demonstrates particularly clearly, the *Metamorphoses* is as interested in the semantic instability of language as it is in the ontological instability of bodies, and endeavours to entangle the two wherever possible in order to demonstrate their mutual implication. In play-ing with the unstable relationship between signifier and signified, Ovid reveals again his affinity with the deconstructive reflexes of post-structuralism, and here puts this linguistic impulse into the service of a highly hospitable theme. There are, moreover, places in this poem where Ovid plays in more radical ways with the relationship between signifier and signified. In his personifications of abstract terms – envy, hunger, sleep and fame – the poet gives concrete body to the names of ideas that do not exist at the level of corporeal substance outside this text. By concretizing these abstractions, and making them readily avail-able to our senses, Ovid conjures tangible referents for terms that might nor-mally be viewed as impoverished in this regard – terms that are traditionally sustained by a surfeit of signifier to signified. Tissol's study helpfully connects the procedures by which Ovid fleshes out these linguistic *phantasiae* to the verbal devices by which he makes other phenomena materialise at the level of

---

123 Tissol 1997.
124 Tissol 1997, 4. The phrase 'mere wit' is that of Otis 1970, 192–193.
125 Tissol 1997, 15–17.
126 Cf. Tissol 1997, 26–29 for discussion of this episode.

language,[127] and thus contributes to those post-structuralist appraisals of the poem that see it as a hospitable vehicle for the view that 'reality' is, more often than not, little more than a rhetorical effect.

The concerns of Rosati and Tissol come together in a work by Philip Hardie, who shares with them an interest in the illusory surface of Ovid's language, and sets out to elucidate this aspect of the *Metamorphoses* further by proffering a theoretical basis for it and by connecting it to the theme of desire that runs through the entirety of Ovid's oeuvre. With *Ovid's Poetics of Illusion*, Hardie traces the strategies that Ovid uses to conjure illusions of presence throughout his literary works, while at the same time deliberately exposing the absences at their core.[128] While Hardie's account of the linguistic foundations of Ovid's equivocation between absence and presence takes its bearings from Derrida's view of the trace,[129] his broader scrutiny of the visual and verbal conjurings of Ovid's poetic imagination shows what these feignings owe to the absences that drive desire, for which Lacan provides the theoretical basis. Hardie explicates his Lacanian model in light of an opposition between the realms of the imaginary, with its promise of presence and plenitude, and the symbolic, which is the register of language, culture, and all that bars us from merging with that state of lost wholeness that we seek in the imaginary.[130] The 'mirror stage' is of course the episode in Lacanian thought that stages for us most memorably the passage that the human subject passes through in order to reach past the imaginary to the symbolic, and Hardie uses this Lacanian paradigm to unpack the dynamics of desire in a number of episodes, including the story of Narcissus.[131] But Hardie also shows what a Lacanian view of the symbolic register of desire might do to help us understand some of the dynamics of Ovid's poem that readers have historically found hardest to stomach. The repetitive nature of Ovid's stories of desire (and rape) is here explained in light of Lacan's view of the linguistic structure of the unconscious, whereby desire moves along the

---

127   Cf. Tissol 1997, 61–88 for an extensive discussion of the different personifications in the *Metamorphoses*.

128   Hardie 2002a.

129   While Hardie 2002a never mentions Derrida explicitly, his discussion of the fictions of presence in the spoken word (at e.g. p. 22) is indebted to arguments made in Fowler (forthcoming), which explicitly channels Derrida's attempt (in Derrida 1967) to counter the metaphysics of presence that dominates western philosophy by making the absences that writing inscribes a precondition of thought and experience (rather than a by-product of it).

130   Fowler 1999, 156–168 offers a Lacanian reading of the Pyramus and Thisbe episode in book 4 along similar Lacanian lines.

131   Hardie 2002a, 143–172 (a revised version of Hardie 1988). Cf. also Butler 2013 for a discussion of the relationship between Ovid's Narcissus and Lacan's mirror stage.

signifying chain in an endless series of metonymies, propelled by the lack on which it is premised but cannot acknowledge.[132] The multiple protagonists of the *Metamorphoses* (or, rather, the absence of a single protagonist) renders the poem's repetitions amenable to being viewed as an allegorisation of this principle of desire in the abstract; for, as Hardie points out, the use that Lacan makes of a linguistic model for the unconscious prioritises the cultural system of language over the individual subject.[133] In making this point, Hardie gestures toward the ideological uses to which Marxist thinkers, such as Althusser and Zizek, put Lacanian thought, without developing this angle in great detail himself.

Hardie's scrutiny of the ideological is limited in this book to considering Ovid's engagement with the illusionistic spectacles of imperial power in the triumph poems of exile,[134] which he reads as an extension of the poet's career-long preoccupation with the illusions of visual representation. Another scholar, Andrew Feldherr, takes the various spectacles of imperial power (e.g. religious sacrifice, the theatre and arena spectacles) as his starting point, and draws on the paradigms of viewing that they entail, before reading these cultural experiences back into the spectacles that Ovid describes in the realm of myth in the *Metamorphoses*.[135] Part of the force of Feldherr's argument resides in the fact that a number of the myths treated by Ovid in the *Metamorphoses* were popular topics of theatrical shows (including mime shows) as well as of mythical reconstructions staged to gruesome effect in the arena.[136] He successfully shows how the reader's experience of these stories from cultural contexts outside the text becomes a necessary component of their experience of reading them in the literary medium of Ovid's epic poem. Ovid's account of the story of Lycaon, which centres on the mal-performance of a sacrifice and which thereby problematises the boundaries between beast, human, and god that sacrifice normally seeks to stabilise, exploits readers' familiarity with this

---

132   Hardie 2002a, 67–68. The assimilation of Ovid's rape narratives to a discourse of desire reinforces the (usually male) aggressor's perspective in these stories, in ways that many feminists are likely to find problematic. Cf. Rimell 2019, 7–8 and esp. n. 31 for discussion of the feminist critique of Lacan in e.g. Irigaray 1985 (the insights of which Rimell 2006 also draws on).

133   Hardie 2002a, 68.

134   Hardie 2002a, 307–315 (cf. my analysis of his discussion on p. 76 below).

135   Feldherr 2010.

136   Coleman 1990 is the *locus classicus* for the topic of 'fatal charades' staged in the Roman arena. The examples of mythological arena enactments that she cites include stagings of the stories of Orpheus and Daedalus. Cf. Feldherr 2010, 172–178 for discussion of the implications of Coleman's reconstruction for the versions of these stories in the *Metamorphoses*.

ritual practice in order to drive home the story's implications for the slippage of these boundaries in the stories of metamorphosis that follow.[137] Feldherr highlights how the visual spectacle of sacrifice invites readers to take up a particular perspective with regard to the sacrificial victim (we either sympathise with it or condemn it as worthy of being sacrificed), and that this model of viewing, which carries over into many of the stories of metamorphosis that follow, lends itself to the hierarchies used in Ovid's day to structure imperial power. This becomes especially stark in the case of the stories that invoke the context of the arena, because of the way in which this cultural institution becomes a direct instrument of imperial power under the Principate. But as Feldherr stresses, the chief contribution that references to the arena make to the *Metamorphoses* is a blurring of the line between fiction and reality, since this is precisely what happens in the 'fatal charades' that are staged as spectacles in and for the arena.

Modes of viewing are likewise the concern of Victoria Rimell's study of the dynamics of intersubjectivity that Ovid explores across his oeuvre, including within the *Metamorphoses*. Her book *Ovid's Lovers*, discussed earlier, inflects the ideological questions that attach to the gaze in Ovid's poem with a specifically gendered dimension, and thus broadens our appreciation of the poem's political implications beyond its immediate historical context.[138] In this study, Rimell supplements those studies of the gaze in the *Metamorphoses* that regard the story of Narcissus as the poem's touchstone, by proffering Medusa as an alternative model of the gaze: an empowered female gaze which holds the power to stun and deaden. Her book draws on the work of Luce Irigaray in order to posit the figure of Medusa as a feminist paradigm, one that embodies the fears that men express in their need to conquer the other via specular duplication, as well as their conception of woman (and especially female genitalia, for which the Medusa head stands as a potent symbol) as somehow outside representation.[139] Rimell unpacks the complex dynamics of the story of Medusa in *Metamorphoses* 4–5,[140] before then showing how her manner of complicating the gaze is itself reduplicated across Ovid's oeuvre where it interlocks with the male gaze in competitive conflict at times. Her reading of the Orpheus episode, in which Orpheus seems to take up the position of Medusa by killing Eurydice the second time around with a (backward) glance,

---

137 Cf. Feldherr 2010, 131–149 for discussion of the significance of the story of Lycaon, and of sacrifice more generally, for his broader argument about spectacle in the *Metamorphoses*.

138 Rimell 2006.

139 Cf. Rimell 2006, 5 and 16 n. 41 for some very suggestive readings of Irigaray in connection with Ovid's Medusa.

140 Cf. Rimell 2006, 1–40 for discussion of this episode.

demonstrates the ambiguities that cut through this passage regarding the true agent (and object) of the gaze, and the implications that this confusion of subject and object has subsequently for Orpheus' sexual identity.[141]

As this brief survey shows, the intellectual prerogatives of post-structuralism, and the aesthetic prerogatives of its broader cultural church, post-modernism, found a highly amenable vehicle in the *Metamorphoses*, and helped to reposition this text at the centre of the Classical literary canon. But after several decades, some of these approaches can seem a little tired when replicated now (however exhilarating the original readings remain), and the scholarship on this author has been calling out for a change of critical direction for some time. One approach that lends itself readily to this text, but which has not yet been applied to it in a truly sustained manner, comes under the sign of posthumanism, a term that might seem to share much in common with post-modernism (and/or post-structuralism) insofar as both are defined by the supplementary 'post-', yet which is in fact resistant to enough of the habits of post-structuralist thought as to mark a discernible break with it. While approaches to and definitions of posthumanism may vary, they share a commitment to displacing the human subject from the position that s/he has long held at the centre of western thought by situating her within broader technical, biological, informatic and economic systems and networks.[142] And while language may be adduced as one such system,[143] it is no longer a privileged one, for a major concern of much posthumanist thought is to move away from humanism's prioritising of language and consciousness and to focus on the continuities between human and other life forms by emphasising the porosity of the human body.[144] The boundaries of the body are easily breached when we situate the human within wider biological and technological forcefields, which are therefore capable of producing the very kinds of ontological change that stories of metamorphosis may be said to allegorise.[145]

---

141   Rimell 2006, 104–122 on Ovid's tale of Orpheus.
142   Among the more commonly cited introductions to posthumanism available, see Hayles 1999; Wolfe 2010; and Braidotti 2013. One of the chief differences between these authors focuses on the extent to which they identify posthumanism with transhumanism (or not). Cf. Wolfe 2010, xii–xiii for discussion.
143   Wolfe 2010, 3–30 puts Derrida's writings on written language (e.g. Derrida 1976 and 1988) in conversation with the systems theory of Luhmann 1995 in a (polemical) attempt to make systems theory and poststructuralism align.
144   In distinguishing his understanding of posthumanism from the transhumanist version that Hayles understands, Wolfe 2010, xv argues that 'fantasies of disembodiment and autonomy' are among the very legacies of humanism that posthumanism proper opposes.
145   Cf. esp. Clarke 2008.

A subset of posthumanism, and one that brings with it an especially urgent political message for our own times, seeks to displace the human from the self-appointed position of domination that s/he has long held over the complex ecological system that we call the environment. Ecocriticism is a heuristic tool that may be aligned with a number of other critical movements. But at a significant point in its development, a vocal contingent of the environmental movement specifically defined its goals in opposition to those of post-structuralism out of a concern to label the environment, and its destruction, as realities rather than simply rhetorical conceits. The post-structuralist bias of Ovidian scholarship of the past thirty years has generated a large number of studies that focus on the rhetorical status of *loci* in the *Metamorphoses*, and on the metapoetic significance of the poem's landscapes.[146] But the poem also speaks to the consequences of human intervention in the environment, for both good and ill, and models for readers a variety of different ways of configuring their relationship with other actors, both human and non-human, within the global ecosystem of which they form part.

This message appears most starkly in the central book of the poem:[147] in book 8, we find juxtaposed in the tales of Philemon and Baucis and Erysichthon a pair of stories that illustrate contrasting attitudes toward the environment, and the consequences of those attitudes.[148] Philemon and Baucis are identified not only by their hospitality and piety toward the gods, but by the extent to which they identify with the environment around them, both before and after their metamorphosis into trees. Religious piety might be expected to find expression in respect for the environment, given traditional Roman beliefs about the *numina* that dwell in features of the natural world. But as Emily Gowers has pointed out in a pivotal reading of the episode, Philemon and Baucis exceed this attitude of traditional respect, by identifying closely with the trees that they are yet to become both in their own physical persons and in the construction of their dwelling.[149] Their story of environmental harmony is made the more memorable by being juxtaposed alongside the

146   E.g. Hinds 2002 (discussed on p. 45 below). Hinds follows a tradition of scholarship established by Segal 1969; and Parry 1966.

147   'Middles' have long been identified as an important site for metapoetry in Latin poetry, where poets like to advertise their stylistic commitments. But Kyriakidis and De Martino 2004 notably include 'content' as well as 'style' as an integral part of the manifesto of the middle.

148   Gowers (forthcoming) also notes the environmental message that this pairing of stories in book 8 loudly transmits for the poem as a whole.

149   Gowers 2005 highlights the ontological fluidity that pervades this episode, as Philemon and Baucis are described as if they were virtually made of wood, along with the rest of their humble wooden dwelling, long before they are changed into trees.

story of Erysichthon, a figure whose destruction of the environment brings about a form of self-destruction that resonates strongly with twenty-first century experiences of the human cost of human-inflicted environmental degradation.[150] The hunger with which Ceres punishes Erysichthon for cutting down her sacred grove is so all-consuming that it leads to Erysichthon's destructive consumption of everything around him, including, finally, his own consumption of himself. This story serves as a powerful parable for the human cost of an environmental destruction that has been caused in our own era by an economic model premised on insatiable consumption, and advertises the *Metamorphoses* as a text that might repay the kinds of scrutiny that contemporary environmental criticism offers.

In the remainder of this section, I will plot one possible route through certain discourses of current environmental criticism and suggest what readings such a route through this critical terrain might open up for the *Metamorphoses* along the way. Neither the sketch of environmental criticism nor my own readings of the *Metamorphoses* are intended to be exhaustive. But they are intended to show how very different a reading of this poem would be that took seriously its environmental content, in comparison with those readings, which have hitherto dominated Ovidian scholarship, that tend to view landscape as little more than a metapoetic trope.[151] The manifold ways in which the *Metamorphoses* answers to different areas of contemporary environmental discourse make this a text that speaks to some of the most pressing existential concerns of our own time.

4   *Metamorphoses* (ii): Naturecultures

At the heart of ecological discourse lies the fraught interrelationship between nature and culture, terms (or concepts) that have long defined themselves against one another, even if various iterations of critical posthumanism have lately attempted to transcend their dualism with the hybrid coinage 'naturecultures'.[152] The difficult relationship between nature and culture lies, in part, in the difficulty of defining what either of these concepts is or means;[153] in

---

150   For a reading of the Erysichthon myth along these lines, see Da Silva 2008.

151   Gowers 2005; Sissa 2019; and Schwindt 2016 are important and exciting exceptions to this prevailing scholarly bias.

152   Haraway 2003; and Latour 2017, 16 (who arranges the terms in a virtually identical formulation: Nature/Culture).

153   This is perhaps particularly true of 'nature' (although Williams 1976, 49–54 describes 'culture' as equally hard to define). Cf. Soper 1995, 1–3; and Morton 2007, 14–15 for different

part, in the very structure of their opposition, since in practice it is all but impossible to separate out the so-called natural from the so-called cultural. If (broadly speaking) nature describes the condition of life, death, nourishment and reproduction that most life forms are born into, while culture denotes the system of codes and conventions that social groups (humans, above all) devise in order to transcend this state, any clear-cut demarcation between the two spheres would seem especially liable to slippage in the age of the Anthropocene, where few if any parts or aspects of the 'natural' world have escaped modification by the impact of human technoscience.[154] And this deconstructive reflex has a less anthropocentric flipside, for just as climate scientists detect the (largely detrimental) influence of human 'culture' everywhere in the natural world, biologists also claim the cultural for plants and non-human animals, which are shown to display forms of conventional behaviour (including modes of semiotic communication) that were once commonly held to be the reserve of human culture.[155]

The nature/culture (nature/human) dualism maps on to a series of other binary sets that are likewise the target of posthumanism's ecological critique.[156] Underlying the nature/culture divide is the more deep-rooted Cartesian dualism of subject and object that underpins the assumptions of human exceptionalism, driving the belief that human subjects can separate themselves off from the natural world, and regard it as an object of their cognition, and, potentially, control.[157] Connected to this one is the opposition between mind and body (and, by extension, between mind and matter),[158] which is similarly

---

views of the reasons for this difficulty.

154   Cf. Heise 2016, 8–10 for a helpful account of the spectrum of different attitudes to this entanglement, from lament (exemplified by e.g. McKibben 1989) to those who critique that lament by showing what it owes to a metaphysical conception of nature as somehow separable from the human (e.g. Cronon 1995).

155   Cf. de Waal 2001; and Fragaszy and Perry 2003 for examples of social learning in non-human animals; and Iovino and Opperman 2014 for a range of different approaches to the storied properties of, and semiotic play within, the material biosphere.

156   Cf. Plumwood 2002, 17 for an eloquent account of the dishonest logic that polarising dualisms are made to serve in the name of opposing nature to reason: "The polarising aspects of dualism involve sorting a field into two homogenised and radically separated classes, typically constructing a false choice between contrasting polarities in a truncated field which can be conceived in much more equal, continuous and overlapping ways."

157   Soper 1995, 42–44 usefully contextualises the Cartesian position in light of a broader scientific revolution underway at the time, which sought to replace an animistic view of nature as 'ensouled' organism with a view of nature that emphasised its inorganic, mechanistic properties.

158   Soper 1995, 43–49 provides a helpful survey of the different ways in which this tension is reconfigured in the philosophical tradition after Descartes, from Kant to Heidegger.

responsible for the perception of the environment (like the body) as inert material, available to be shaped and manipulated by the dynamic force of human reason and science.[159] And characterising all these oppositions is the inevitable gender distinction, according to which 'nature' is identified with the embodied female, and the science that has systematically violated it belongs to the principle of disembodied male rationality.[160] A series of binary pairs, then, that have been used to organise and/or explain the historical relationship between human subjects and the environment in the modern era,[161] and to account for the deleterious impact that humans have had on the environment throughout this period.

The structure and power dynamics of this set of oppositions have been targeted recently from a number of different positions and within a variety of different discourses, any number of which may be (and have been) harnessed by the environmental movement in its concern to restore some form of ecological equilibrium. The so-called New Materialisms inherit from their Marxist forerunners the need to reposition the human subject in light of object forces, which are here conceived of not as socio-economic currents but in the most literal sense: as powers emanating from and exerted by phenomena traditionally perceived as objects.[162] Agency, according to this model, is not in the exclusive domain of the human but is distributed throughout networks or assemblages consisting of a wide array of different phenomena, including human beings, but also such disparate actants as chemicals, genes,

---

159 Plumwood 2002, 15 describes the opposition thus: "The ecological crisis is the crisis of a cultural mind that cannot acknowledge and adapt itself properly to its material body, the embodied and ecological base it draws on in the long-denied counter-sphere of 'nature.'" As her argument progresses, it becomes clear that it is not 'reason' *per se* that she blames for this crisis, but the systems of power (e.g. Capitalism) that have enlisted it as part of the polarising strategies that underpin their hegemonic visions.

160 Plumwood 1993 is the classic account of this view. See also Grosz 1993.

161 The opposition between 'the human' and 'the environment' is in itself a problematic one from an ecological perspective, and is the target of a cogent critique in Alaimo 2010, which promotes the view that humans (or human bodies, at least) *are* (part of) the environment. See pp. 51–52 below for discussion.

162 'New Materialisms' is the catch-all term commonly used to refer to the variety of materialist approaches that have been developed since the mid-80s with a view to eliding distinctions between animate and inanimate matter. These include, among others, the technological transformation of genetic matter advanced in the cyborg visions of Donna Haraway's feminist engagement with the natural sciences in Haraway 1985; the concept of 'agential realism' developed by the physicist-feminist Karen Barad in Barad 2007; the Deleuzian inflected 'Vibrant Matter' of Jane Bennett 2010; and the Object-Oriented-Ontologies advanced by Harman 2002, and developed by Bryant, Harman and Smicek 2011 (as well as by Morton 2013).

technologies and climatic atmosphere. The structuring principle of the dual is here displaced by the more distributive structure of the network, which has an incidentally distributive effect on the category of the human, who is shown to consist herself of a variety of different elements and actants. The idea of the assemblage is indebted, in part, to Bruno Latour's Actor Network Theory, which seeks to democratise agency at the phenomenal level by re-situating the human within networks that consist of an array of different phenomena, and recasting 'the social' of social science as a relation between 'things' as well as people.[163] This egalitarian view of distributed agency is likewise on display in the work of Donna Haraway, who first coined the term 'naturecultures' in *The Companion Species Manifesto*, according to which different species (including the human) have forever co-existed and co-evolved interactively with one another, in ways that make it very difficult to say where the human and non-human (or 'nature' and 'culture') definitively begin and end.[164] Haraway's manifesto for recalibrating the hierarchical relationships between species (in this instance, between humans and dogs) is of a piece with the democratising goals of Latour's project. For at stake in the fiercely contested stories of canine evolution that she relates is not only, 'the relation between what counts as nature and what counts as culture in Western discourse and its cousins,' as Haraway puts it, but also, 'the correlated issue of who and what counts as an actor.'[165]

In its staging of the process whereby humans turn into alternative (that is, non-human) life forms, the *Metamorphoses* presents a parable of sorts for the procedures whereby the human and non-human, culture and nature relate to and become entangled with one another.[166] Up until this point of his career,

---

163   Latour 1987; and 2005.

164   Haraway 2003, 25–32. Haraway's case study in this manifesto is the relationship between humans and dogs, which as she shows, have depended on one another and shaped the evolution of each other's species throughout their shared history. The popular myth of canine origins, in which the human domesticated the wolf and, in doing so, 'created' the dog, offers a paradigmatic example of the traditionally conceived relationship of nature and culture, in which the human acts on the passive objects of nature in order to make them instruments of cultural, human intention. Against this account, Haraway proffers an alternative set of evolutionary tales, in which canine opportunism first drove the dog (or lupine proto-dog) to live alongside the human in order to avail itself of the 'calorie bonanzas provided by humans' waste dumps.' Humans may have subsequently affected canine evolution considerably (by controlling dogs' reproduction, among other means), but they will in turn have been biologically altered themselves as a species by living alongside dogs, in a process that Haraway, following Lynn Margulis, calls symbiogenesis.

165   Haraway 2003, 26.

166   Pythagoras' speech in *Met.* 15, long dismissed by scholars as a humorous interlude, is now being reclaimed by scholars with posthumanist interests (e.g. Sissa 2019) as the culminating manifesto of this view.

Ovid had been the poet of *cultus*: elegy is, as we have seen, an urban genre, and in Ovid's hands especially so. The worst insult he can lay at a Roman male is to call him *rusticus*. Yet the *Metamorphoses* marks a break with this bias. It shows us little of the urbane world of elegy, and instead depicts the human – men and women – interacting with phenomena of the natural world. But what does nature – *natura* – mean for an ancient Roman? Or for a twenty-first century English speaker, for that matter? Raymond Williams famously remarked that the word 'nature' is probably the most complex word in the English language;[167] and the same may be true of its Latin counterpart *natura* for ancient Roman culture. It is certainly just as slippery in its semantic possibilities (if, perhaps, not quite as contested in its ideological baggage), as the range of its uses in the *Metamorphoses* testifies.

The English word 'nature' is also highly culturally and historically specific: as Leo Marx has shown in his discussion of the idea of nature in America, the different values that this term accrues in the course of U.S. history are thoroughly implicated in the question of this country's national identity, and are informed as much by the mythology of the American frontier as they are by the different religious and philosophical movements situated in the U.S. at different times.[168] 'Nature' may describe a geographical terrain, as it did for the founding fathers who discovered, upon landing in Cape Cod, an inhospitable wilderness that mapped easily onto their religious ideas of nature as fallen.[169] It may define the essential properties of an object. Or, through a process of metonymy, it may describe a physical principle ('the laws of nature'), according to which the material world as we know it (including humans) operates (Newtonian physics, for example, or Darwin's theory of Natural Selection); or a metaphysical idea that provides an abstract account for why it should operate in this way, and which gives (non-human) agency to the creation and regulation of the cosmos.[170] Alternatively, through a process of metaphorical extension (referred to as the 'naturalization of the social'), it may be used to prescribe (the thoroughly cultural) norms or conventions that conservative reactionaries customarily tell people they ought to live by. In practice, the distinctions between these different usages are sometimes difficult to sustain. The question of whether subscribing to a particular physical principle of nature eradicates

---

167   Williams 1976, 219–224, where he also claims that any history of the term would also be a
        history of a large part of human thought.

168   Marx 2008.

169   Marx 2008, 10.

170   Williams 1976, 220 argues that one can trace a precise history for the abstract singular
        Nature (of science or metaphysics) from the specific singular ('the nature of something')
        insofar as it tracks the emergence of a singular God from *a god* or *the gods*.

an assumed metaphysical principle was one that worried Darwin, who anticipated the way in which understanding the scientific laws of nature might
remove the metaphysical need for god.[171] But it is equally possible to view science as providing a metaphysical substitute for god, a secular religion of its
own; the ambivalence of this question may have been somewhat familiar to
Epicureans in Ovid's own day.[172]

The *Metamorphoses* concerns itself with the abstraction of *natura* to a
degree that is unusual for an epic poem. While the term *natura* arises only
once in the *Aeneid*, it occurs over thirty times in the *Metamorphoses*, with a
prominence that signals the strong line of genealogical filiation that connects
Ovid's text with the materialist poetics of the *de Rerum Natura*.[173] But where
in Lucretius' poem *natura* is invested with a consistent meaning, standing in,
as it does, for a cosmic system built on the principles of atomic physics, in
Ovid's pluralistic universe, by contrast, it features in a range of different discursive contexts. In the poem's opening account of creation, for example, we are
told that, when chaos reigned and before the world was divided into different
regions, there was a single face of nature in the world (*unus erat toto naturae
vultus in orbe*).[174] A few lines later, we are told that it was god or 'better nature'
who separated out the warring elements of this primordial soup.[175] A little
later on in the book, following Ovid's account of the flood, we are told that the
stones that Pyrrha and Deucalian throw over their shoulders acquire a softer
nature as they turn from stone to flesh.[176] *Natura* as the (personified, in this
instance) manifestation of the physical world, *natura* as a metaphysical principle of cosmic order, and *natura* as the property of a living being (or the guar-
antor of that being's properties): three different ideas of nature appear within

---

171   Darwin's anticipation of the public's reluctance to renounce their assumption that Nature
       is separate from the human, and of the atheism that his theory would validate, is well
       noted by Marx 2008, 12–13.

172   Cf. Gale 1994, 208–223 on the role of Venus in the proem to DRN 1, whose attributes are
       subsequently allocated to the scientific principle of *Natura* as the poem progresses. Yet
       this very process might seem to cast *Natura* as more of a metaphysical than a scientific
       principle, along the interpretive lines of *l'anti-Lucrèce chez Lucrèce* coined by Patin 1868.
       Of course, we have no way of knowing how ancient readers would have read the palimp-
       sestic relationship between Venus and *Natura* in the DRN.

173   On the direct significance of Lucretius' DRN for new materialist thought, cf. Serres 1977;
       and Bennett 2004. See also Tutrone 2020 for a view of embodied cognition in the DRN
       that sets Lucretius' thought against traditions of Cartesian dualism. I am indebted to the
       anonymous reader for these references and for the broader point about the significance
       of Lucretius' materialist philosophy for this aspect of Ovid's poem.

174   *Met.* 1.5.

175   *Met.* 1.21: *hanc deus et melior litem natura diremit.*

176   *Met.* 1.403: *mox ubi creverunt naturaque mitior illis / contigit ...*

fairly quick succession of each other in this opening book, all under the same term *natura*. Later on in the *Metamorphoses*, we see *natura* fulfilling another familiar discursive role in the context of a discussion about sexual norms: the term clusters in book 10, within the monologues in which Myrrha wrestles with herself over the question of whether her sexual desires are in accordance with or against nature.[177] And in book 15, it clusters again in Pythagoras' speech in another familiar role – that of the transcendent, metaphysical principle, analogous to (or interchangeable with) god.[178] The range of uses to which we find Ovid putting the term *natura* therefore conforms almost uncannily with the range of uses to which the English term nature is put in modern parlance, and in this sense might seem to bear out Timothy Morton's critique of nature as, 'an arbitrary rhetorical construct, empty of independent, genuine existence behind or beyond the texts we create about it,' and, perhaps because of this, an easy repository for reactionary ideologies.[179] Yet while we do not need an idea of 'nature' in order to recuperate the ecological dimension of Ovid's poem, we do need something like it in order to view metamorphosis through the lens of naturecultures. 'Nature,' like most other things, means next to nothing in isolation. It only comes to mean in relation to other terms and ideas. What matters for our purposes is what and how it means in dialogue with culture. If Ovid's conception of *natura* is revealed to be non-essentializing by virtue of the sheer diversity of his usage of this term, this is only fitting for a concept that we want to see in dialogue with an idea of culture that is equally versatile.

An earlier generation of structuralist critics taught us to believe that in the Greek conceptual tradition that Ovid inherits, the nature-culture divide is articulated as a distinction between civilisation (the world of man-made laws, language and social conventions that culminates in the civic organization of the polis), and the untamed wilderness that lies (or should lie) outside it – a schema that found fertile ground in Greek tragedy.[180] Ovid's poem is less interested in the city state, its foundations and organising structures, than in the wilderness that lies beyond, in ways that mark a clear and deliberate break

---

177   Of the seven occurrences of the term in *Met.* 10, three of them appear in the Myrrha episode, either as part of Orpheus' commentary on the taboo that Myrrha breaks in the story, or as part of her own monologue to herself (*Met.* 10.304–353).

178   Cf. esp. *Met.* 15.104, 253 and 354. Throughout Pythagoras' speech (and in the prelude to it at *Met.* 15.60–74) we find a recapitulation of many ideas about *natura* that we first glimpsed in the opening book.

179   Morton 2007, 21–22.

180   Segal 1981, which opens by describing Greek tragedy against a contrast drawn between the perfect Doric temple at Bassae, and the wilderness around it, exemplifies this approach (which originates with e.g. Vernant and Vidal-Naquet 1972).

with his immediate epic predecessor, Virgil. One of the few ktistic legends that Ovid includes in his poem concerns the foundation of Thebes, the city that had long provided Athenian drama with a site for imagining its darkest fears and fantasies about selfhood, sovereignty and family relationships – the very issues where the overlap between nature and culture becomes most fraught. Typically, much of Ovid's treatment of this city's mythical foundations takes place in a wilderness: if Greek tragedy normally deconstructs the nature/culture divide by staging the incursion of nature into culture, then in Ovid's reading of tragic Thebes, this dynamic is reversed.

The episode begins by identifying Cadmus, the human founder of Thebes, as the traditional culture hero, when he kills the monstrous snake who resides as a pestilence on the future site of the city. Yet, as Philip Hardie has shown in a classic reading of the episode, far from successfully imposing culture on nature by ridding Thebes of its resident monster, Cadmus' heroic actions only sow the seeds, quite literally, of the snake's bestial legacy in the form of la bête humaine, when he sows its teeth in the earth and these produce a race of spontaneously warring soldiers.[181] The population of Thebes descend from the five warriors who survived this, and the protagonists of the subsequent stories within this larger Theban history remind us of their snake-born forefathers at various points. The story concludes with the transformation of Cadmus and Harmony into snakes, in a move that takes us back full circle to the episode's start, and might seem to offer a neat reversal of its moral, by turning the culture hero into the same earthly creature that he first slew. Yet the snakes that Cadmus and Harmony become are benign to humans; and when Cadmus slithers over Harmonia, prior to her own transformation, the action materializes an all too human affection for the wife from whom he resists being parted (Ovid surely knew that snakes do not mate for life).[182] The narrator's final comment is that the two must have found some consolation for their serpentine shape in the knowledge that their grandson (Dionysus) was worshipped throughout India as well as Greece.[183] This altruism for the human species they have left behind, in recognition of the benefits that Dionysus, the culture-giver, has bestowed on mankind as a result of their sacrifice, separates their nature from that of a credible snake, and identifies them as humans in snake bodies. If Cadmus the

---

181   Hardie 1990, 225.

182   The naturalcultural implications of this scene are underscored by its allusion to the scene in *Aeneid* 7, in which Amata is driven mad by a snake planted on her body by the fury Allecto. In converting metaphors into new realities, Ovid domesticates Virgil's snake, retaining the sexual component of the Virgilian scene (cf. esp. *Met.* 4.595–599), but removing its association with Dionysiac frenzy.

183   *Met.* 4.604–606.

culture-giver becomes part of *natura*, the snake that in this context symbolizes *natura* has been acculturated – or humanized, at least. 'Nature' is transformed by its contact with human culture, and vice versa.

Ovid's meditation on the interrelationship between nature and culture in this episode is not limited to the plight of Cadmus or even of Thebes. A number of the individual episodes that make up Ovid's Theban History take place in a wilderness and provide another site for reflecting on the relationship between nature and culture in the transformation that the landscape itself undergoes as a result of the metamorphoses that take place within it. The process of enculturation that we see these landscapes undergoing as a result of human contact taps into a familiar environmental discourse concerning the role that wilderness plays in the western imagination, and the place that it occupies on a spectrum between nature and culture. But it also stimulates further environmental questions concerning the extent to which we are (part of) 'the environment,' or exceptional agents within it who act upon it more than we are acted upon by it. Wilderness, as many environmental critics have shown, is not a transhistorical category, but comes loaded with different ideologies in different historical periods and places.[184] In Ovid's poem, the wilderness that I refer to has a quite specific hue: it is the *locus amoenus*, the 'pleasant place' which derives from a number of literary traditions,[185] and which is characterised above all as untouched by human hands. This is likewise the essential feature of modern 'wilderness' narratives, the principle on which their dualistic vision always depends. In Ovid's particular vision, the *locus amoenus*, although a place of pristine beauty, is also repeatedly the site of violence and, more specifically, sexual violation. This narrative pattern lends the landscape a sinister quality, as we come to identify it as the recurrent setting for a rape. But it also nuances the common environmental position that identifies the human as nature's perpetual aggressor, for in these stories, the victims are humans. The landscape in which the rapes occur stands in some other relation, whether one of symbolic affinity with the human victim, or as part of the agency that performs the act of violence upon them. Within the story of Salmacis and Hermaphroditus, for example, Salmacis, the nymph who rapes Hermaphroditus, is coterminous

---

184   The classic analysis of these is Cronon 1996. For a wider collection of perspectives on this issue, see Cronon 1995.

185   Many of these traditions, which include 'pastoral' (or, at least, Virgil's *Eclogues*), tragedy (or, at least, the opening scene of Euripides' *Hippolytus*), epic (or, at least, certain scenes from the *Odyssey*) and lyric (especially Sappho and Ibycus) are listed piecemeal throughout Segal 1969. But there is still scope for a more systematic analysis of how Ovid brings the various elements of these traditions together in his own formula for the *locus amoenus*.

with the pond that forms a central component of the *locus amoenus* landscape that lures Hermaphroditus in. By contrast, in Ovid's account of the rape of Proserpina, the unplucked flowers that form part of the opening scene stand in symbolic affinity with the girl's virginity.

The *locus amoenus* is instantly identifiable because its description is highly formulaic, as Stephen Hinds has brilliantly shown, and is commonly treated as a rhetorical *topos* – a classic example of a landscape description that turns landscape into 'landscape', a rhetorical construction that draws attention to its own artifice.[186] This rhetorical quality might seem to identify Ovid's wilderness as an emphatically literary place. Yet the 'wilderness' understood by environmental discourse is likewise a highly cultural, artificial construction. Unsurprisingly, perhaps, it shares a number of features with the *locus amoenus*. Attending to the formulaic components of the *locus amoenus* allows us to map Ovid's wilderness discourse quite precisely onto that of modern environmental criticism. The *locus amoenus* is, for example, commonly introduced by a *locus est* ('There is a place ...') formula. The *locus* may be replaced with a substitutive term designating a more particular place (a *lacus*, for example, or a *lucus*). But the present tense of *est* is unchanging, to the extent that this itself becomes a trope that Ovid plays with and parodies.[187] The *locus amoenus* exists in an eternal present up until the point at which human actors intrude. A similar point is made by William Cronon about the place that wilderness occupies in the modern (and not so modern) western imagination. As he puts it, 'In virtually all of its manifestations, wilderness represents a flight from history. Seen as the original garden, it is a place outside of time from which human beings had to be ejected before the world of history could properly begin. Seen as the frontier, it is a savage world at the dawn of civilization, whose transformation represents the very beginning of the national historical epic ... Seen as the sacred sublime, it is the home of a God who transcends history by standing as the One who remains untouched and unchanged by time's arrow. No matter what the angle from which we regard it, wilderness offers us an illusion that we can escape the cares and troubles of the world in which our past has ensnared us.'[188] What is instructive about the version of the wilderness narrative that Ovid gives us with the *locus amoenus* is that it plots the process of enculturation whereby the pristine landscape, once touched by human contact, enters historical time. This is thematised for us most dramatically in the story of Proserpina, which

---

186 Hinds 2002.
187 The example that Hinds 2002, 127 gives is in fact taken from the *Heroides* (*Her.* 12.67–69).
188 Cronon 1996, 16. Cf. Gifford 2016 for a Classicist's take on what this tradition of wilderness writing owes to ancient pastoral.

opens with a *locus amoenus* that exists in a perpetual spring,[189] but which ends
with the creation of seasons that will take this landscape (and all others) into
the differentiated temporality of the seasonal year.[190]

But time itself is a product of naturecultures as much as anything else, and
seasonal time no less than any other kind. What is left opaque in Ovid's version of this story in the *Metamorphoses* is the role that humans have to play
in the creation of the seasons: in the version of this story that Ovid gives us
in the *Fasti*, it serves as an aetiology of the plough, and hence of the role that
agriculture plays in marking (and creating) seasonal time.[191] This *aetion* is
barely visible in the version of the story that we find in the *Metamorphoses*,
where agriculture is scarcely mentioned at all. Yet it may be there under erasure: for the rape that Proserpina suffers may be read in symbolic terms as a
metaphor for the violence meted on the landscape through agriculture, and in
this sense may be an important aspect of the story's latent meaning. Given that
the advent of agriculture is sometimes taken as the starting point for the age
of the Anthropocene,[192] modern readers may incline to read the fact that it is
Dis who performs this foundational rape of nature as a comment on humanity's death drive. More explicit is the gendered significance of this scene. The
view of nature as virginal terrain to be 'mastered' by humans, who are cast
collectively as male, is a common trope of western traditions of nature writing, as is the casting of nature as a nurturing mother. What has been less discussed, as Soper highlights, are the Oedipal tensions generated by 'mastering'
a landscape that may be virginal terrain and nurturing mother at one and the
same time.[193] This tension is staged for us quite openly in this story, where
both mother and daughter feature as analogues of the landscape: Proserpina
the figure for the virginal land, untouched by the plough; and Ceres, goddess
of agriculture, and source of earth's bounty, who responds to the rape by with-
holding that bounty – or rendering her fructifying land still-born.

If the versions of the *locus amoenus* that we find in the *Metamorphoses*
invite us to plot the process whereby nature and culture become entangled, the
poem also depicts situations that pitch the two against one another, in which
human figures are overshadowed – and even eliminated – by the natural environment in which they find themselves. The New Materialisms provide tools

---

189   The eternal present of this *locus amoenus* is thus stated twice (Met. 5. 385–391): *haud
        procul Hennaeis* **lacus est** *a moenibus altae, / nomine Pergus, aquae ... * **perpetuum ver est.**

190   Cf. *Met.* 5.565–567.

191   Cf. *Fasti* 4.559–560.

192   Cf. Ruddiman 2003; and Crutzen and Steffen 2003 for discussion of when the
        Anthropocene may have begun.

193   Soper 1995, 105–107.

for explicating this mode of alienation, encompassing as they do philosophies such as object-oriented-ontology wherein any idea of human agency is all but obliterated by being placed in relation to the greater power and longevity of natural or naturalcultural objects.[194] The aesthetic responses generated by this harder, object-oriented form of materialist thought link up with a much older tradition of criticism on the sublime which is firmly at home in certain modes of nature writing – above all, those that emphasise the sublime power of the natural landscape, and the awe and even terror it inspires in the human subject who passes through it.[195] This tradition of writing is familiar to many readers and writers of modern eco-criticism from the Romantic poets and above all the work of William Wordsworth,[196] but it has an analogue in Classical literature, and is equally well-known to readers of Lucretius and Virgil.[197] It is manifested too in Ovid's *Metamorphoses*, where, as ever, it appears in especially exaggerated form: in book two, Phaethon's chariot ride has been placed by scholars within the rhetorical traditions of the ancient sublime,[198] and demonstrates well the affinities that such traditions share with the prerogatives of the new object-oriented ontologies. These affinities have been highlighted recently by James Porter, who builds on his work on the ancient material sublime by arguing that the project of many traditions of ancient philosophy, from the pre-Socratics to the Stoicism of Marcus Aurelius, is to forge an ethical relationship not to one's self (*pace* Foucault) but to, 'the blank contingency and indifference of the world', a project that they share in practice (if not in theory) with the object orientations of today's New Materialists.[199] The Phaethon myth, which was sometimes read in antiquity as an allegory of the Stoic theory of ekpyrosis – whereby the world and all its contents were periodically destroyed by fire at the end of every Great Year prior to being born again – presents a compelling further illustration of Porter's argument. Phaethon's experience of terror when confronted by his own inability to control the laws of nature might well

---

194   Harman 2018; and Morton 2013.

195   Cronon 1996, 10–13 usefully situates approaches to nature in the nineteenth century that may be gathered under the sign of the Romantic sublime within a longer history of western attitudes to wilderness.

196   Cf. Weiskel 1976 for an account of the Romantic Sublime that connects this movement to its ancient literary roots in Longinus *et al.*

197   Porter 2016, 445–516 cites a series of Latin poets, from Lucretius and Virgil to the Aetna poet, as notable contributors to the tradition of the material sublime in ancient literature.

198   Schiesaro 2014, 86–87 for a discussion of what Ovid's account of Phaethon's journey owes to discourses of the sublime. Schiesaro highlights points of contact between Ovid's Phaethon narrative and Longinus' reference to Euripides' description of the same journey, from his tragedy of Phaethon, which he cites as an instance of the sublime.

199   Porter 2019.

be taken to mirror our own feelings of self-destitution in the face of the abyssal nature of global warming, an event that humans have caused but over which we appear to have no control. The objects (or hyperobjects) of nature (and/ or natureculture) dwarf the human, and confront us with the limits of our own agency, even (and perhaps especially) when we are directly implicated in their making.[200]

The example of Phaethon stands at one end of the symbiotic relationship between nature and culture that the *Metamorphoses* stages, demonstrating the erasure of the human that follows on from attempts to separate nature off from culture and submit it to forms of human intervention and control; the rape of the land by man-made agriculture in the Proserpina myth stands at another. But between these two poles we encounter a spectrum of different bonds conjoining nature and culture in the poem with varying degrees of harmony or friction. Sexual and/or marital metaphors feature prominently in the depiction of these entanglements of nature and culture, and, as such, conform to the emphases of environmental discourse which deploys a similar cast of figurative terms to depict the commingling of different species. Rape is but one of the sexual paradigms available. In her account of the traditional story that humans have told themselves about how the dog was created by domesticating the wolf, Donna Haraway uses an alternative sexual metaphor in order to capture the auto-erotic narcissism of the story: 'Humanist technophiliacs depict domestication as the paradigmatic act of masculine self-birthing, whereby man makes himself repetitively as he invents (creates) his tools. The domestic animal is the epoch-changing tool, realizing human intention in the flesh, in a dogsbody version of onanism.'[201] This image stands in direct contrast to the dominant sexual paradigm of *Companion Species*, which shares with Haraway's earlier manifesto on cyborgs a commitment to unsettling traditional gender identities in the name of queer ecologies, by focusing in this instance on the queer marriage that is the relationship between a woman and the dog she lives with. The treatise begins with an account of the bacteria that Haraway and her dog must now share as a result of the saliva they have exchanged in their interspecies kisses, and celebrates the 'significant otherness' of companion species such as humans and dogs, in a playful queering of the clichéd term for a spouse in the most traditional heteronormative relationship.[202] The queerness

---

200   Global warming is, according to Timothy Morton 2013, 27–30, a good example of a hyper-object: a phenomenon so massively distributed in time and space relative to the human that we cannot perceive it directly.

201   Haraway 2003, 27.

202   Cf. Haraway 2003, 6–10 for a summary of the chief philosophical and sociological influ-ences on her concept of significant otherness. These include: Whitehead 1929 on process

of their marriage resides in part in the fact that it is non-reproductive, and this forms a central part of the ecological commitments latent in her inter-species manifesto, which are articulated elsewhere in the slogan to 'make kin, not babies!'[203]

Haraway's account of how companion species constitute one another, through cohabitation, co-evolution, and cross-species sociality, presents a powerful template for thinking about cross-species metamorphosis in Ovid's epic poem. In concrete terms, it finds analogues in the story of Philemon and Baucis, who are transformed into different species of tree, an oak and a linden, which lean on one another in quasi-marital support, in a perfect illustration of ecological queering, their cross-species otherness a nod to the cooperative, ostensibly non-reproductive aspect of the marriage that they shared when they existed in human form. In the story of Cadmus and Harmony, by contrast, the erotic love that Cadmus, as a snake, demonstrates for Harmony, when still a human, is a catalyst for her metamorphosis into the same species. While Daphne, as laurel, remains beloved of Apollo and is made one of his abiding cultural signifiers, regardless of her own ongoing resistance to this cross-species alliance. Ovid's version of significant otherness demonstrates the frictions that may subsist across species in such queer marriages, as well as the love and even erotics that such encounters may sustain.

In this way, the *Metamorphoses* highlights for us a minor problem in Haraway's approach, by virtue of the range of different species that Ovid manages to incorporate into his narrative of cross-species exchange: for all her protestations that the insights presented in *The Companion Species Manifesto* hold for cross-species relationships other than just humans and dogs, her discussion never ranges beyond the specifics of this relationship, and make one wonder what an account of the significant Otherness between the human and the rat would look like.[204] For these too are companion species, but companions

---

ontologies; Verran 2001 on emergent ontologies (that is, the practices that arise out of attempts made by different cultures operating in a post-colonial context to forge a conjoined future out of their disparate inherited histories); Thompson 2005 on ontological choreographies (an idea that emerges from her work on the new categories of kin that assisted reproductive technologies make); and Strathern 1991 on partial connections. These disparate discourses are connected by the interest that they all take in how to relate across cultural and biological differences, even if those differences are confined to the human species. Haraway's conception of significant otherness draws on and extends these philosophies by applying their anthropological insights to relationships between different species.

203   Haraway 2016, 102.

204   Haraway 2010, with its focus on spiders and other 'critters', offers a significant corrective to her earlier work in this respect, and suggests a promising avenue for future work on the

with whom it is harder to identify a mutually affirming affinity. Much of the value of Ovid's poem for ecological discourse is that it supplements (or extends) Haraway's approach by describing a vast range of different ways of relating across species, including indifference and open hostility, and thereby displaces the human from the kind of cross-species relationships which serve to reinforce its special privileges. The *Metamorphoses* reminds us that even the dog, that most companionable of species, holds affinities for the human that range beyond the kind of affectionate interdependence that Haraway describes. Actaeon's dogs, for example, domesticated and obedient to their human master, cannot recognise or sympathise with him when that humanity is suspended, and remind the (human) reader of how cruelly prejudicial its alliances with domestic species are against those species that are excluded from its special cross-species relationships. Ovid's Hecuba, meanwhile, taps into a tradition of canine representation in which the dog stands on the outer perimeter of culture's dialogue with nature, the mother who becomes savage in defence (or, in this case, vengeance) of her young.[205] Her transformation into a dog is preceded by an act of savagery that makes her resemble the wild cur familiar from taunts on the Homeric battlefield, the warrior-dog polluted by contact with quantities of human blood.[206] It is also preceded by her transformation from queen into slave, a shift in status that is easily accommodated to the colonial slur that equates the subjugated with the (undifferentiated) animal Other.[207] Hecuba becomes both metaphorical dog and metaphorical animal long before she literally materializes into one. And we are left wondering about the literalness of that materialization, since it is never described for us as an externally observed event. Perhaps the metaphorical transformation was the only one that ever happened. And perhaps it is the only one that really matters.[208] By inviting us to observe the opaque line between literal and metaphorical metamorphosis, Ovid demonstrates how little separates us from the non-human animals that humans choose to define themselves against.

    Metamorphoses.

205   Cf. Franco 2014, 108–112.

206   As Holmes 2015, 33 n. 10 points out in her study of naturecultures in the *Iliad*, the dog stands on the (dark) side of nature in the classic, if dualistic, discussion of nature and culture in the *Iliad* by Redfield 1975, 193–199.

207   This idea underpins much of the argument in Spivak 1988. Cf. also Derrida 2002, 392–403 for further reflections on the various forms of problematic authority that are invoked by differentiating between 'Human' and 'Animal'.

208   Cf. Barkan 1986, 23 on how metamorphoses in the *Metamorphoses* 'make flesh' of metaphors.

Haraway's work forms part of a larger tradition of humanistic thought on animals, which provides a rich set of tools for scrutinizing the relationship that Ovid draws between physical metamorphosis and the affective, dispositional and behavioural resemblances that inhere between human and non-human animals. But the poem also contains stories that answer readily to some of the more materialist approaches of ecological discourse – approaches that efface the boundary between the human and non-human by focusing on physical (and chemical) components that are shared by both. One approach that falls into this category, and which lends itself particularly readily to stories of metamorphosis, is that developed by Stacey Alaimo in *Bodily Natures*.[209] In this work, Alaimo seeks to deconstruct the distinction between 'the human' and 'the environment', by casting a spotlight on the human body as an interface for the transit of other non-human natures and *corpora* (the bacteria on the tongue of Haraway's dog, for example, or the DNA transfected through her saliva), and thereby identifying the human in this corporeal sense as an integral part of the environment.[210] 'Trans-corporeality', the term that Alaimo coins to describe the material interconnections and exchanges that occur between human and other bodies, emphasises how, in its physical encounter with other material substances and corpora, the human body not only affects these other bodies, but is itself affected and transformed by them.[211] This model of interaction complicates the question of human agency considerably. For example, Alaimo's focus on 'toxic bodies' (that is, human bodies that are so permeated with man-made toxins that they may be viewed as hazardous to others) reveals the human to be both subject and object of toxic harm. On the one hand, the substances that threaten most harm in modernity's 'risk society' are made by humans, a feat that would appear to cast the human in the familiar role of aggressor. On the other, Alaimo's study focuses on the human victims of toxicity, victims who are objectified both by toxic substances and by the socio-economic forces that place them in the pathway of those substances, since historically the burden of toxic suffering has been borne by members

---

209   Alaimo 2010.

210   Like Haraway's, Alaimo's work reacts to a tradition of feminism that sought to disentangle the female from nature by de-emphasising her biology and emphasising instead the social construction of gender. Alaimo's own response to biological determinism is not to reject biology *tout court* by bracketing the body, but rather to challenge the idea that biology is fixed.

211   Again, queer theory is invoked as inspiration for this procedure. Yet *Bodily Natures* expands its inquiry beyond questions of sex and gender by considering the range of different ways in which bodily transformations occur as a result of contact with other actants: by ingesting contaminated food, for example, or by absorbing chemicals and toxins that linger on the ground, in the water or in the air.

of economically disadvantaged communities, frequently people of colour.[212] But a victim of toxicity may in turn inflict involuntary harm by transferring toxins from their body to the bodies of those with whom they subsequently come into contact. Thus even as Alaimo's study reasserts the death of the subject by equating the human with its material body, it nevertheless highlights the new forms of (harmful) agency that the human body can take on when situated within toxic networks.

Ovid's poem contains some striking scenes in which human actors experience toxicity and see their bodies monstrously transfigured as a result. Even if the poem offers little meditation on the social and racial inequalities involved in actual (as opposed to imaginative) toxic environments, these scenes do call our attention to the particular modes of human suffering experienced in such situations, and to the unequal power relations that they inscribe. *Metamorphoses* 14 opens with a toxic narrative, when Circe the witch, rebuffed by the sea-god Glaucus, takes her revenge on the object of his desire, a nymph named Scylla, by laying a noxious trap for her that transforms her into the monster with whom we are familiar from Homer's *Odyssey*. Ovid's account of this metamorphosis, which is thoroughly focalised through the incredulous eyes of Scylla (even if it is not actually narrated in her first person voice) shares points of contact with Alaimo's discussion of 'material memoirs,' autobiographical accounts of experiencing disease in a 'risk society,' in which a narrator recounts their discovery of a physical problem within their own body that seems to have been caused by toxic factors outside it in their environment. Alaimo highlights how the narrating subject within these memoirs is transformed by the discovery that, 'the very substance of the self is interconnected with vast networks of biological, economic, and industrial systems that can never be entirely mapped or understood.'[213] Within this genre of memoir, which mixes scientific knowledge with autobiographical personal history, 'the self becomes unrecognisable ... not because of its discursive construction, but

---

212   Alaimo's focus on the human victims of toxicity (as opposed to the 'natural environment', which is the more common focus of environmentalist concern) makes her study an example of what Buell 1998 calls 'toxic discourse,' a tradition of writing that stems from Carson 1962, and which is now strongly associated with environmental justice movements. This tradition of writing (and acting) provides an important corrective to the deep ecologist's view that 'the human' is only ever the environmental aggressor by highlighting the social and racial inequalities entailed in environmental suffering: Bullard 1990 is the seminal account of 'environmental racism' in America. Cf. also Guha and Martinez-Alier 1997; and Nixon 2011 for wider perspectives on the disproportionate environmental suffering inflicted on the global south.

213   Alaimo 2010, 23.

because self-knowledge in risk society demands "scientific" understanding of a vast, coextensive materiality.'[214]

As Alaimo highlights, capturing the multiple strands of these material agencies is no easy task. One reflex that narrators of material memoirs sometimes resort to is to divide the narrating from the narrated self in order to convey the sense of self-alienation that entails from the discovery that one's 'self' belongs to impersonal forces outside one's own understanding or control. Ovid's account of Scylla's transformation into a monster conforms, to some extent, with this reflex. Incredulous over her transformation, she tries to run from the dogs who now form part of her own body; and when she looks for her 'own' body parts, she finds the space that they should occupy populated by these same dogs. The description conveys the degree of self-alienation entailed in discovering that your body has been taken over by bodies that are not your own.[215] This example of transcorporeality is all the more conspicuous in Ovid's poem because the metamorphosis is not complete: becoming monstrous means retaining a hybrid form. For Scylla this means retaining not only the faculties but part of the form that she had before. However fabulous her metamorphosis, it stands in allegorically for stories of disease in which subjects experience the horror of seeing their bodies playing host to other malignant bodies. In the case of diseases caused by toxic environments, 'playing host' is the apposite phrase, since the diseases are felt to come from outside, even if it is hard to locate their exact point of origin. But, of course, this transformation serves as a prelude to the harm that Scylla will subsequently inflict on others who come within distance of her (even if this part of her story is not recounted explicitly within the *Metamorphoses*), in a final twist in the tale of her toxic agency.

Alaimo's move to make matter and bodies matter is part of a larger materialist turn at work in the humanities, which has sought to recuperate various

---

214   Alaimo 2010, 24. While the narrative of Scylla's transformation in *Met.* 14 does not obviously channel scientific discourse, the narrative of Glaucus' metamorphosis at the end of *Met.* 13 (which *is* notably written in the first person, and which serves as a prelude to the account of Scylla's transformation in the following book insofar as it is similarly brought about by the absorption – or in this case ingestion – of toxic herbs), channels a range of specialist discourses, esp. religious purification and magical practice, at *Met.* 13.951–957, which have an equally alienating effect. Cf. Hopkinson 2000 *ad loc.* for the details.

215   Cf. *Met.* 14.61–65: ... *ac primo credens non corporis illas / esse sui partes, refugitque abigitque timetque / ora proterva canum, sed quos fugit, attrahit una / et corpus quaerens femorum crurumque pedumque / Cerbereos rictus pro partibus invenit illis* ('... and at first not believing that these are parts of her own body, she flees in fear and tries to drive away the boisterous barking things. But what she flees, she takes along with her; and feeling for her thighs, her legs, her feet, she finds in place of these only gaping dogs' heads, such as Cerberus might have.')

objects and substances that the discursive preferences of post-structuralism disavowed.[216] Within environmental studies, the question of whether nature exists as 'discourse' or as prediscursive reality is a particularly fraught one. Much of the political polemic of an earlier generation of deep ecologists devolved from an outright hostility to the discursive accent of post-structuralism, which held (or was assumed to hold) that nature could never be more than a rhetorical conceit.[217] But the idea of nature as a determining reality has had an equally contentious past, as discourses of sex and gender show.[218] Proponents of naturecultures tend to take a flexible approach to the discursive and/or material status of environmental phenomena, as befits their understanding that most of these phenomena are the products of 'nature' and 'culture' simultaneously. Yet this understanding places an unusual burden on its practitioners since it requires them to subscribe to disparate disciplinary epistemologies that frequently make contradictory claims to truth. As Bruno Latour points out in his account of the contending discourses of which science studies currently consists, the hole in the ozone layer is both 'too social and too narrated to be truly natural;' yet it is, at the same time, 'too real and too social to boil down to meaning effects.'[219] A product of the networks of natureculture such as this is both 'simultaneously real, like nature, narrated like discourse, and collective, like society,' and requires us to be able to inhabit these disparate discourses, and hold their various – and inevitably contending – truths in our heads at one and the same time.

So too, I would argue, for Ovid: nature is not only a rhetorical trope (although it may be this too). But the *Metamorphoses* also offers a range of insights into the formation and workings of ecological systems and naturecultures, which draw on a variety of different discourses – scientific, philosophical and poetic – for their description,[220] and place a similar mode of epistemological burden on readers as the one identified by Latour for practitioners of contemporary science studies. Scholars have long noted the references to different philosophical schools and materialist accounts of *natura* at work in the

216   Alaimo 2010, 6: "What has been most notably excluded by the 'primacy of the cultural' and the turn toward the linguistic and the discursive is the 'stuff' of matter." As she points out, current attempts to recuperate the material world are either built on philosophies (by e.g. Spinoza and Deleuze) that are frequently read as counter-currents to the linguistic turn, or on re-evaluations of the work of theorists at the heart of post-structuralism.

217   Cf. e.g. Slocombe 2005, 494.

218   Cf. Dollimore 1991, 114–115 on the violence perpetrated against homosexuality in the name of 'nature'.

219   Latour 1993, 6.

220   Myers 1994 provides the most thorough account currently available of these discourses.

account of creation in *Metamorphoses* 1, a plurality that we might put down to the poet's Hellenistic preference for offering multiple explanations.[221] But this may likewise be viewed as an excellent example of the very pluralism that Latour has in mind when explaining the need to break with the hard categories of thought that modernity ushered in, and restore a degree of flexibility to our ways of accounting for the world that is perhaps more familiar to scholars of the so-called 'pre-modern.'

5   Ovid's *Fasti* and the Ideological Bind

If the *Metamorphoses* is receptive to contemporary environmental discourses, the political implications of these discourses arguably speak more to the concerns of modern readers than of ancient ones. Viewed within its own context, 'the political' in Ovid's oeuvre (when it extends beyond the questions of personal identity that scholarship on the amatory works and *Metamorphoses* touches on) has generally been taken to mean 'Augustan ideology.' And more often than not, readings that focus on Augustan ideology come to centre on ambiguities over the degree of subversion present in the text. The *Fasti* has been an especially powerful magnet for such readings over the past thirty years, and provides an excellent illustration of their interpretive possibilities as well as their constraints.[222] In this section, I offer a review of some of these readings of the poem's engagement with Augustan discourse, before then suggesting an alternative approach to questions of ideology in my reading of the exile poetry in the section that follows.

A foundational point of reference for any discussion of the politics of Augustan literature (and of the politics of reading it) in the past thirty years is an essay published in 1992 by Duncan Kennedy, in which he applied his distinctive deconstructive scalpel to the oppositional terminology that critics commonly used to describe those politics: the opposition 'Augustan' and 'anti-Augustan', is, as Kennedy shows, deeply unstable, since each term is only ever

---

221   The opening account of creation out of chaos gestures in turn to Stoic, Epicurean and Empedoclean systems of thought, before then moving into the realm of mythography with the Hesiodic Myth of Ages etc. Cf. Myers 1994, 41–44 for discussion.

222   Ovid's amatory works have also attracted extensive scrutiny over the years for the evidence they provide of Ovid's attitude toward Augustan policy, esp. regarding his anti-adultery laws. Cf. Davis 2006 for a helpful overview. And *Tristia* 2 has seemed to many to represent Ovid's most direct address to the emperor. Cf. Barchiesi 1993 = 2001, 79–104; and Gibson 1999 for alternative readings of the subversive potential of that text, and of the alibis that the poet builds into it to deflect any actual charges of subversion.

made meaningful from its dialogue with the other, and thereby incorporates that other into its 'own' field of meaning. 'Discourse,' writes Kennedy, 'as well as being an effect and instrument of power, is at the same time a focus for resistance and subversion.'[223] Augustan discourse is therefore constituted as much by the anti-Augustan voices that seem to oppose it, as by those that appear to prop it up, such that the texts and other cultural productions that get bundled under each of these labels may become interchangeable. One opposition that is commonly enlisted by scholars of Augustan poetry to deconstruct this pairing of political terms is that provided by literary genre: epic and elegy would seem to map onto the opposition 'Augustan' and 'anti-Augustan' in a fairly straightforward way, and yet this opposition is as susceptible to deconstruction as the political ideology that it is commonly made to carry.

Ovid's *Fasti* became a particularly important site for the consideration of this set of issues in the 90s.[224] An elegiac poem about the Roman calendar, which had recently been reformed by Augustus and now bore the mark of many of his religious reforms as well as commemorating the events of his rise to power in a number of its anniversaries, the *Fasti* appears to take elegy out of the countercultural field of *amor* and into the official Augustan domain of religion, history and politics. Yet the elegiac genre of the *Fasti* brings with it a horizon of expectations that cannot help but shape its content: Ovid is self-conscious about making his couplets bear the strain of material that is too weighty for them to carry, and modifies his ostensibly anti-elegiac material to the aesthetic (and ideological) expectations of his metre.[225] Mars is programmatically de-armed at the start of *Fasti* 3 in order to accommodate him to his elegiac context.[226] At the same time, the religious focus of the *Fasti* generates a new opposition between the *arma* of epic and the *ara* (and *sidera*) of this poem, content that situates it within a venerable Hesiodic tradition (which had in the Hellenistic period accommodated both epic and elegy).[227] This opposition is represented in the poem by the figures of the martial Romulus and the religious Numa, and is the source of another set of tensions for Augustan ideology that Kennedy and others painstakingly deconstruct.[228]

---

223   Kennedy 1992, 40.

224   Ovid's *Fasti* is one of a constellation of texts that Kennedy 1992, 42–47 draws on to demonstrate how Augustan discourse deconstructs the opposition war/peace. Hinds 1992 offers a comparable set of reflections in his study of the ideology of genre in the *Fasti*.

225   Cf. esp. *F.* 2.3–8 and *F.* 119–126, with Hinds 1992, 83–85 for discussion.

226   Cf. Hinds 1992, 88 on the significance of *F.* 3.1–8.

227   Hinds 1992, 113–116.

228   Cf. Kennedy 1992, 45–47; and Hinds 1992, 113–153 for extensive discussion.

But the deconstructive reflexes of scholarship on the *Fasti* are particularly stark because of the way in which they came in the 1990s to focus specifically on an opposition generated by structuralist linguistics. In 1987, Mary Beard published a highly influential essay on the Roman calendar, in which she drew on Saussurean linguistics in order to describe the calendar's distinctive manner of organizing history under the banner of ritual. In this piece, Beard deploys Saussure's distinction between syntagmatic relations (which is to say, the sense carried by a unit of language in a linear sequence), and paradigmatic (or, more accurately, associative) relations (which is to say, the sense carried by a verbal unit in relation to other units of the same category that may substitute for it) in order to demonstrate a crucial distinction between a calendar like the Christian one and that which operates in Republican Rome.[229] In the Christian calendar, a single narrative (the life of Jesus Christ) runs through the liturgical year; each ritual thus gains meaning from the position it holds in relation to the rituals that are contiguous with it, which form part of a single, continuous story. With the Republican Roman calendar, by contrast, festivals generate meaning from the new associations that they accrue over the course of historical time, and function as sites of commemorative substitution.

The example that Beard chooses to illustrate the Roman calendar's paradigmatic axis of organization is the *Parilia*, a festival which is commonly celebrated as the 'birthday' of Rome – the day on which the city walls were first founded. But as many sources note, it also appears to be a pastoral festival that predates this civic milestone: a festival in honour of the goddess Pales, when herds and flocks underwent a process of ritual purification. And as Beard further points out, it continued to accrue associations in the late Republic, when it became the appointed day for celebrating games to commemorate the announcement of Caesar's victory at Munda.[230] In Beard's striking formulation, each festival in the Roman calendar is a pageant of Roman history, in which different moments and events from Rome's past jostle against one another and compete for attention in the ritual performance of that particular day. While Beard's model for the Roman calendar is drawn from structuralist linguistics, there is a deconstructive reflex to her analysis, insofar as she is at pains to stress how a single festival may carry multiple 'meanings' and implies that the associations drawn from one event in its history may carry over to characterise another.

---

229 Beard 1987, 7–8 cites Saussure 1983, 121–125 for the opposition between syntagmatic relations and paradigmatic associations.

230 Beard 1987, 9 cites Dio *Histories* 43.42.3 for evidence of this celebration, but notes that the games commemorating this event soon fell out of use.

Beard's approach to the calendar proved to be of central importance for subsequent scholarship on Ovid's *Fasti*, which sought to demonstrate how Ovid manipulates the alternative syntagmatic and paradigmatic axes via which individual calendar units may generate meaning in order to produce certain ideological effects. The ostensible freedom of associations that the calendar affords in its alternative axes of organization presents the poet with the opportunity to select material in the service of his own commentary on contemporary politics. At the same time, the calendar itself provides him with a screen behind which he can veil his ideological agenda, by downplaying the choices it affords and suggesting that he is simply following the calendar's own template. The first exemplar of this approach was Byron Harries who, in a pair of articles, set out to demonstrate the liberties that Ovid takes in selecting events from Roman history and juxtaposing them alongside others in his narrative of the calendar year, as well as pointing up the relative compression or expansion of his narrative treatment of a given event.[231] In her article, Beard had emphasised the paradigmatic axis of the Roman calendar, and had viewed syntagmatic relations as a prerogative of calendars that tell a single story across the year. Harries picks up on the structuring principle of the syntagma, and shows that it too was something available to the poet to manipulate – not by isolating a single narrative from Roman history and narrating this across the calendar year; but by recognising that, in a linear poetic treatment of the poem like Ovid's *Fasti*, the selection and juxtaposition of material in contiguous calendar units (or even as part of the same unit) could generate certain effects (or 'counter-effects').[232] The example that Harries chooses to illustrate this point is the juxtaposition of the extended syncrisis comparing Augustus with Jupiter as well as Romulus in his entry for the Nones of February (*F.* 2.119–144), the anniversary of the date on which Augustus received the title *pater patriae*, alongside the erotic image of Ganymede that appears as part of the astrological entry for the same day.[233] Harries suggests that this image, with its reminder of Jupiter's sexual misdemeanours, serves to deflate the image of Jupiter against whom Augustus has just been compared, with a concomitant set of effects on the characterisation of Augustus himself.[234]

The approach developed by Harries was subsequently picked up and expanded by Alessandro Barchiesi in a book-length study that offers our most

---

231   Harries 1989 and 1991.
232   These effects are arguably more visible in an edition such as that of Heyworth 2017 which prints the text as continuous, without the epigraphic headings for different days that break up the text in earlier editions.
233   Harries 1989, 166–167.
234   Barchiesi 1997a, 81–83 submits the same juxtaposition to an alternative interpretation.

extensive treatment of the ideological commentary that Ovid's poem writes on the Roman calendar.[235] Barchiesi discusses the particular syntagmatic tensions (or counter-effects) that Harries discusses and adds to them.[236] But he also returns to the paradigmatic axis of selection and substitution that Beard stresses in her original article and shows that this too is available to be manipulated by the poet in the service of his commentary on the calendar's ideological script. Ovid's entry for the Quirinalia, on 17th February, for example, reminds readers that this is also the date of the Feast of Fools.[237] The poet appears to have no control over the coincidence of this combination of festivals on a single calendar unit, it is simply 'there' in the calendar. But he can (and does) control which aetiological *causae* to emphasise in his entries for these festivals. Barchiesi shows that Ovid's decision to commemorate the apotheosis of Romulus on this date, a story that tests credulity in many ways, is a choice that may not be determined in any straightforward way by the calendar. In making this story share the same calendar space as 'All Fools' Day', the poet draws on the associations of the latter festival to comment on the gullible fools that the apotheosis story told to explain the Quirinalia makes of readers.[238] This example is illustrative of a broader tendency that Barchiesi seeks to elucidate in his analysis of Ovid's manipulation of the calendar's paradigmatic strata, which come to polarise between two layers: that which evolved over the long Republican period, and the thin overlay of Augustan religious discourse.[239] The identification of Quirinus with Romulus forms part of the latter, such that the effect of the associations that are ushered in by the *feriae stultorum* has an inevitably subversive charge.

In her original article, Beard emphasises that it is the flexibility of the Roman calendar's paradigmatic axis which enables it to accommodate the new festivals of the early principate with such ease.[240] However, she stops short of considering what the effect of this influx of new festivals in celebration of a single dynasty has on the calendar after the fact of their incursion. An important insight of Barchiesi's book is to point out that this flood of new

---

235   Barchiesi 1994b, which was published in English as Barchiesi 1997a.

236   Barchiesi 1997a, 79–104.

237   Barchiesi 1997a, 112–119.

238   Barchiesi, 1997a, 118–119.

239   Barchiesi 1997a, 123–130 offers as his chief example of this Ovid's entry for the Ides of March, which is both the date of the popular Republican festival of Anna Perenna, and the anniversary of Caesar's murder, which Ovid commemorates by describing the slaughter at Philippi to which it gives rise. Although these two events are quite distinct, Ovid's narration of them contains sinister imagistic links.

240   Beard 1987, 11.

imperial festivals transforms the Roman calendar into one that resembles the Christian calendar, with its single liturgical narrative, which Beard had posited as an alternative calendar model.[241] Barchiesi shows how one way in which Ovid's poem reflects this new narrative in the first six months that it covers is in the figure of Romulus, with whom Augustus identifies closely, and whose life narrative comes to unusual prominence in this text.[242] Ovid goes out of his way in *Fasti* 4 to provide a genealogy that links the Julian family not just to Augustus but to Romulus as well.[243] He then refracts the narrative of the imperial dynasty in the life story of Romulus, Rome's original founder. But Romulus is a controversial figure, a bandit and a fratricide, and this gives the poet a leeway to emphasise certain ambiguities in his behaviour, ambiguities that cannot help but cast their associations on Augustus, whom Romulus is there in the text to mirror.[244]

An additional feature of this text to which Harries and Barchiesi both draw attention, and which is also highlighted by Carole Newlands in her monograph on the poem, is the extent to which Ovid occludes his own powers of selection and organization by portraying himself deferring to the gods and other interlocutors whom he consults for information.[245] Yet these divine interlocutors are frequently shown to be unreliable sources, not least because they are highly partial witnesses to the stories that they tell about themselves. In a number of cases, their explanations are either patently untrue or at least not authoritative: the etymology that Flora gives for her name (from *chloris*) runs against the grain of its more obvious derivation from *flos*.[246] On other occasions, Ovid's divine interlocutors draw attention to their own discreditable status as sources

---

241   Barchiesi 1997a, 142–143. In a separate essay, Barchiesi 1997b, 199 proffers this as a possible (and highly plausible) reason as to why the *Fasti* appears to be incomplete: the months of July, August and September are so replete with festivals commemorating important dates in the career of Augustus as to make Ovid's poetic task impossible. The silence left by his text's incompletion of these months is deafening.

242   Barchiesi 1997a, 143–144.

243   *F.* 4.27–60, with Barchiesi 1997a, 172–173. Barchiesi's argument concerning the significance of the genealogy that Ovid provides to link Romulus with Augustus gains additional weight from the important insight of Feeney 2007, 174 that one of the major changes that Augustus made to the orientation of historical time was to supplement the consular *Fasti* with reminders of the number of years that had elapsed since Romulus' founding of Rome in 752 BCE.

244   Cf. Barchiesi 1997a, 155–159 on the intertextual resonance of the verb *indoluit* used to describe Romulus' pique at losing the wrestling contest to Remus at *F.* 2.377–378; and Barchiesi 1997a, 159–164 on Romulus' crocodile tears in reaction to the death of his brother on his own orders.

245   Harries 1989, 171–182; Barchiesi 1997a, 181–213; Newlands 1995, 51–86.

246   Barchiesi 1997a, 189–191.

of falsehood rather than truth: Mercury offers an implausible account of the origins of the Lemuria in an exchange with the poet in which he also reveals his propensity for deception.[247] Ovid's reliance on these would-be sources of authoritative utterance has the effect of casting doubt on the *causae* behind the rituals that his poem records, producing an epistemological uncertainty, which as Carole Newlands suggests, increases as the poem unfolds.[248] The last two books of the poem (books 5 and 6) begin by depicting the poet inquiring into the etymology of the month in question in a conversation with certain divine interlocutors, which, in each case breaks down into disagreement without offering any provisional resolution. Newlands relates this increasing epistemological uncertainty to the premature ending of the poem, by suggesting that it draws attention to the question of how the poem can continue. When we recall the central argument of Beard's article on the Roman calendar, which suggested that it was precisely the profusion of associations and historical events that enabled a given festival to generate meanings, it is striking to note how the need to decide between such events becomes fraught in Ovid's poem. It is not the multiplicity of associations that the festivals and months carry that is, in itself, problematic, but the need for certain authoritative sources to assert the correctness of their explanation over one another. We might therefore reframe Newlands' conclusion by suggesting that it is not the poem's increasing epistemological uncertainty that makes its continuation difficult, but its increasing insistence on certainty.

Another opposition in the poem that both Barchiesi and Newlands set out to deconstruct is the distinction between two different modes of religious discourse: the official new discourse instantiated by Augustus' religious reforms, and embodied in the transformations that certain deities such as Mars and Vesta underwent at this time; and the 'popular' religion associated with Priapus, Flora and the *silvestria numina* associated with Rome's rustic prehistory. Ovid incorporates both categories of religious discourse into his poem, and sets them alongside one another. In his hands, the elements of popular religion are frequently represented by stories of sexual comedy, and draw on narrative patterns derived from Greek satyr play. Barchiesi notes that the chief function of satyr play in its Attic context was to parody tragedy, and demonstrates how this parodic function remains operative in Ovid's text, where the comic interludes that these stories provide serve to deflate the official discourses placed alongside them. More insidiously, both Newlands and Barchiesi highlight how the satyric/Priapic element infiltrates Ovid's entries for festivals that feature

247   Harries 1997a, 177–180; and Barchiesi 1997a, 120–121.
248   Newlands 1995, 79–86.

the newly transformed deities sanctioned by official Augustan discourse, as if to remind readers that these gods have a past that precedes their Augustan makeover, and that that religious past could not be more at odds with the pre-rogatives of the new religious discourse. Mars is not only portrayed as the god of Augustan vengeance, but as the victim of a plot of sexual deception when he attempts to seduce Minerva, and ends up in bed with an old woman in disguise. Most prominently, Vesta, a goddess who, in Augustan discourse, was made to embody the virtue of chastity as well as a number of other Roman ideals, is made the target of an attempted rape by Priapus, who is forestalled and inter-rupted by the braying of a donkey. This farcical story, which ostensibly serves to explain why the donkey is sacred to Vesta, is also a reminder of the popular, Republican view of the goddess in which she is identified with the lower social classes (represented by her affiliation with bakers) in a time before Augustus. Given the way in which the past is frequently invoked as a source of authority in this poem, stories like this highlight the tensions that may arise from bring-ing the past up against the alternative authority of the Augustan present.

Between them, Harries, Barchiesi, and Newlands identify a series of impor-tant oppositions in the structure of Ovid's *Fasti*, and set about deconstructing them with the aim of showing how the poet destabilises many of the assumed certainties of Augustan discourse, and of demonstrating how complex that discourse is. Far from being 'out there,' somewhere beyond this particular text, Augustan discourse is constituted precisely by texts like Ovid's *Fasti*, along with the calendars to be found inscribed in and around Rome at this time, and all the other textual and monumental traces that Augustus and those contemporaries who construct him leave behind. Elegy is, as Kennedy writes, oppositional, and the readings that these scholars proffer focus precisely on the poem's oppositional stance: on the subversive commentary that the poet writes on Augustus' religious and calendar reforms. Yet this commentary is, as they suggest, integral rather than extraneous to Augustan discourse, since opposing the regime is a necessary way of defining it. Having said that, their focus on the poem's critical side ends up reinforcing the opposition that they seek to deconstruct: the familiar method of deconstruction is to destabi-lize one set of polarities to the extent that it generates a new set, and so on *ad infinitum*. But these readings seem to get stuck on the Augustan/anti-Augustan bind that such deconstructive methods should displace. This marks a radical point of contrast with scholarship on other texts from this period, e.g. the *Aeneid*, for which subversive readings are now deemed restrictive and are, because of this, no longer in vogue. Scholarship on the *Fasti*, constrained as it is by an overfamiliar Augustan/anti-Augustan bind, is in this sense still excep-tional, and might be ready for a critical shift.

One route out of this interpretive straitjacket would be to focus on the experience of time that the *Fasti* encodes: Molly Pasco-Pranger suggests one way of doing this, by drawing attention to the different social experiences of time that are witnessed by the poem's reference to a number of different types of calendar, from star charts and menologia to military calendars and the local calendars of different Italian towns.[249] All these speak to the alternative ways in which different social groups may experience time, and provide a salutary reminder that the 'official' Roman calendar is but one time-keeping device among many. Along complementary lines, Angeline Chiu's study of the poem focuses on the representation of women in the *Fasti*, demonstrating how their prominence within this text serves to complicate the overwhelmingly masculine picture of Roman identity that we derive from other sources on the history of Rome and its festivals.[250] In the course of demonstrating this, she also highlights the prominent place given to female religious observances and practices in Ovid's version of the Roman calendar, and thereby shows how his poem draws attention to Roman women's experience of calendar time. Studies like these offer a salutary reminder of the fact that different social groups, and different individuals, will experience time differently. For Ovid's most extensive meditation on this idea, however, we will need to turn to the exile poetry, which, as Denis Feeney has suggested, fills in for the six months of the calendar that are left unwritten in the *Fasti*.[251]

6   Hauntologies of Exile: *Tristia* and *Epistulae ex Ponto*

The sense of belatedness that characterises all of Ovid's works up to and including the *Metamorphoses* assumes a new point of departure and a new complexion in his exilic *corpus*. The *Tristia* and the *Epistulae ex Ponto* not only rework literary traditions that precede Ovid; they are also haunted, above all, by his own preceding literary output: with the *Ars Amatoria*, which is identified from the start of the *Tristia* as a major cause of Ovid's exile, and with the *Metamorphoses*, which represents the high point in his literary career against which he now measures (repeatedly) his literary and personal fall. The exilic works are unusual in that they reverse the expressions of self-confidence that dominate his preceding oeuvre, and articulate instead a poetics of self-deprecation and despair. For this reason, they were slower to receive the

---

249   Pasco-Pranger 2006.
250   Chiu 2016.
251   Feeney 1992.

critical acclaim that greeted his other literary works in recent scholarship, as, for many years, critics took at face value the negative assessment that Ovid himself offers of his exile poetry and assumed the accuracy of that assessment to be self-evident.[252]

Yet the resurgence of interest in Ovid that began in the 1980s did touch on the *Tristia* (the *ex Ponto* a little less),[253] and has continued to build over the years to some extent.[254] The recuperation of the *Tristia* as a poem 'worthy' of Ovid's literary genius began with Stephen Hinds' 1987 reading of *Tristia* 1, in which he unpacks the self-reflexive subtleties of the poet's description of his earlier literary works in this book of poems. Hinds subsequently built on this approach with a series of articles that show how in his exile poetry Ovid revises positions that he had taken in previous works (his treatment of time, for example, in the *Metamorphoses*;[255] or of catalogues of women in the *Heroides*).[256] This approach was broadened by Gareth Williams, whose 1994 monograph likewise sees through the postures of literary decline to reveal the allusive complexity of a wide range of poems in the *Tristia*; and whose 1996 study of the *Ibis* unpacks the layers of Callimachean allusion in this under-read poem.[257] At stake in these studies is a mission to locate in Ovid's exile poetry a degree of qualitative continuity with his preceding oeuvre, by revealing them to be as intertextually rich and self-conscious as his earlier works. Other critics have developed a complementary line of approach by positing points of thematic continuity for the exilic *corpus* as well: Hardie, for example, sees the repeated expressions of longing for Rome that we find in the *Tristia* and *ex Ponto* as an extension of the discourse of desire that runs through Ovid's erotic poetry as well as the *Metamorphoses*, one that substitutes Rome for the various libidinal objects of these earlier erotic texts, and which similarly puts repetition in

---

252   Williams 1994 describes the negative appraisals of earlier scholarship on the exile poetry but delicately resists citing names. Cf. Kenney 1965, 37 for some more concrete examples of the negative view.

253   Or rather, critical appreciation of the *Epistulae ex Ponto* has lagged behind the *Tristia*, in dutiful obedience to the logic of sequels. Renewed interest in the *ex Ponto* is best witnessed by the appearance of a spate of excellent commentaries on the poem: e.g. Galasso 1995; Gaertner 2005; and Tissol 2014.

254   If we were to measure critical recuperation by the emergence of edited volumes devoted to the literary work in question, Ovid's exile poetry fares well: cf. Williams and Walker 1997; and Ingleheart 2011 for appraisals of the reception of Ovid's exile in later (postclassical) literary history.

255   Hinds 1999a.

256   Hinds 1999b.

257   Williams 1996. See also now Schiesaro 2011; and Krasne 2012 and 2016.

the service of desire.[258] Others have shown how the condition of exile is itself anticipated in Ovid's earlier works – above all, in the *Metamorphoses*, which stages the very process of transformation from one state into another as a form of self-alienation.[259]

Yet while these (and other) continuities undoubtedly inhere between Ovid's pre- and post-exilic works, we should not understate the break that exile brings to his oeuvre,[260] since it contains an important political charge. Ovid's exile poetry is defined, most obviously, by the poet's spatial separation from Rome. Yet the poet's enforced removal from Rome is an event, one that has the significant retrospective effect of marking off all of Ovid's preceding career as pre-exilic.[261] This procedure exerts an interpretive pressure on these pre-exilic works as readers look back and see how the new themes of spatial and political alienation were always already literary preoccupations from the very outset of his career. We invariably read the preceding oeuvre differently after exile.[262] There is, moreover, an important political dimension to Ovid's desire to write exile as an event and turning point, a temporal, as much as a spatial, rupture. By the time that Ovid started writing the *Tristia*, there were no other poets of equal fame alive in Rome. He is the 'last of the (major) Augustans', and as such, he could count on the fact that his poetry offered the most authoritative literary record of this moment. There are simply no other literary voices of comparable fame to compete with his, as is clear from the poem that closes his literary *corpus* (whether or not by his own design), *ex P.* 4.16, in which Ovid situates himself within a canon of contemporary Tiberian writers, most of whom are all but unknown to us. The nine books of exile poetry, which are thought to span

258   Hardie 2002a, 285–292.

259   Cf. esp. Fulkerson 2016.

260   Regardless of whether or not the poet was actually exiled. Arguments given by e.g. Fitton Brown 1985 for the possibility that Ovid was not exiled include the dearth of testimony by other contemporary or near contemporary writers, as well as the unreality of Ovid's description of Tomis. But the idea that Ovid's exile is a fiction is no longer widely accepted. Cf. Williams 1996, 3–7 for a more sophisticated appreciation of the 'unreality effect' of Ovid's descriptions of Tomis.

261   A point made eloquently by Henderson 1997, 148: "From now on, Augustus had determined, all 'Ovid' was to be exilic, whether 'pre-', 'post-' or indeterminably caught by exile – the catch-all instant that at once oriented the whole of his story around its forcefield."

262   Some critics (e.g. Ingleheart 2006; and Giusti 2018) take this procedure a step further, attributing the new hermeneutic lens that exile casts over his preceding literary career to Ovid's own authorial hand, as they view the scenes that anticipate his later exilic preoccupations as the result of a process of rewriting from exile (an argument that can fall prey to a form of intentionalist fallacy as critics attempt to reify their exilic readings of a text by attributing them to the hand of its author).

a nine-year period, serve to characterise this moment as a time of cultural and political barrenness – when poets no longer enjoyed free speech, and when the most exciting event happening on the Roman literary landscape was the slow emergence of these books of exile, monotonous in their theme and despairing in their sentiment. These books stand as a deliberate rebuke to the emperor and to the imperial system that Ovid was in the unique position of being able to provide a lasting record. For this period, the closing years of Augustus' rule and onset of Tiberius', marks the emergence of the principate as a political system – as more than a one-off case of one-man rule, maintained by Augustus' unique political talents. It is only with the peaceful accession of his appointed heir that the mode of rule that Augustus had fashioned is revealed to be the monarchy that it is. The 'excessive' writing that Ovid embarks on in exile there-fore has a performative aspect:[263] the poetics of negation that lies at the heart of Ovid's repetitious exilic project spells out the aesthetic consequences of the new political regime.

The melancholic retrospection of the exile poetry, the various forms that this retrospection takes, and the media that it presupposes resonate today with a term that music and other cultural critics have used to describe a com-parable retrospective trend in our contemporary cultural landscape, one that they too invest (and see as invested) with a similar melancholia. 'Hauntology' is a term coined by Derrida to describe the spectral quality that characterises moments of historical disjunction, when agencies of the virtual act on events without actually existing, or 'haunt' them in the manner of ghosts.[264] The term describes a concept (or 'puncept') that takes its bearings from the term ontology, yet which refuses the premises of that term by positing not an idea of being, and the self-presence that is implicit in that idea, but the quality of non-being that is peculiar to ghosts, which paradoxically 'return' to the present from the past.[265] Derrida's particular objective in this work was to describe the way in which various spectres of Marx (and of Marxism) continued to haunt the hegemonic neo-liberal order of the late 1990s, which had been heralded

---

263   'Excessive Writing: Ovid in Exile' was the title of a conference devoted to Ovid's exile poetry that took place at the Freie Universität, Berlin, in December 2017.

264   Derrida 1994 draws on the spectral imagery that Marx had himself used to refer to the spectre of Communism haunting Europe in the opening sentence of *The Communist Manifesto*.

265   Derrida 1994, 10. As Hägglund 2008, 82 puts it: "What is important about the figure of the spectre is that it cannot be fully present: it has no being in itself but marks a relation to what is no longer or not yet." The 'not yet' of Hägglund's formulation helps to bring out how hauntology differs from Derrida's earlier ideas of non-being like the trace, specifi-cally because of its relation to the future as well as the past.

by some as an 'end' of history, but which, as he points out, only qualifies for this description in an ideal sense (at best).[266] Marxism may therefore be identified as an example in itself of an agency of the virtual in this era of late Capitalism, as may many of the financial abstractions that define the period of its spectral return.[267]

Spectres of Marx was written in and for a particular historical context; yet its hauntological implications have persisted well into the present, as Derrida's arguments continue to haunt political and cultural discourse, in ways that may make us wonder whether we are living suspended in the same spectral moment of history. In the 2010s, for example, 'hauntology' was taken up by a number of popular music journalists and practitioners to describe the sonic landscape of that moment and connect it to historical conditions that Derrida had been describing over fifteen years earlier, as if those conditions had barely changed.[268] But hauntology is an idea that translates to other eras too. My contention in this section is that the late-Augustan/early Tiberian age, for which Ovid's exile poetry provides a unique witness, qualifies as a similarly spectral historical (dis)juncture; and that Ovid's poetry from this period may be read as a cultural product of this hauntological moment. Admittedly, the historical conditions that give rise to this ancient work are very different from those that underpin the popular cultural productions of today. Yet there are parallels between the respective moments to which they belong, which may account for their comparable cultural effects. For if the moment that Derrida describes is one haunted by the spectres of Marxism, which is declared dead only to carry on haunting the Capitalist realism of the present with reminders of the paradoxes and inconsistencies on which its economic triumphalism is premised, so the advent of monarchy in Rome is similarly haunted by the Republic that it displaces:[269] the new monarchical system retains the constitutional trappings of the old republican one, which now provide a persistent reminder of how

---

266   The fall of the Berlin wall was expected to bring about the end of Communism, yet (Derrida implies) the spectre of Communism continued (and continues) to haunt Europe and the west as Marx had himself predicted, and is likely to do so as long as the contradictions on which Capitalism is premised are there to be exposed. Cf. Derrida 1994, 100–104 for a list of ten of these contradictions, or, as he describes them, 'the plagues of the new world order.'

267   One such economic spectre would be capital itself, which acts on the future (in the form of e.g. derivatives contracts) without existing as anything other than an abstraction. Cf. Derrida 1994, 156–221 on the spectralization of capital and the commodity form.

268   Cf. esp. Fisher 2014; and Reynolds 2011.

269   Just as the Republic is haunted by the pre-Republican monarchy that it displaces. My thanks to the anonymous reader for this point.

meaningless these legal frameworks have become, and which will haunt the new system with that realization in perpetuity.[270]

Ovid's exile poetry presents one of our earliest meditations on this paradox. The haunting of the new political system by the old is made especially apparent in the *Epistulae ex Ponto*, which consists of letters addressed to a variety of named individuals from prominent senatorial families in Rome, who are here assembled in the virtual space of the letter collection. If Cicero's letters present us with a scenario in which letters are used to conduct the business of statecraft, either as a supplement or substitute for the exchanges that take place in the Curia and Forum, the *Epistulae ex Ponto* continues the project begun by Horace in his first book of *Epistles* of disembedding the letter from these networks of 'live' political discourse. But where Horace's letters depict an idealised 'empire of letters', in which the industry of the emperor has left Horace's elite patrons 'free' from the Curia to reflect on higher things, Ovid's *ex Ponto* presents a different kind of imperial dynamic, wherein Ovid's elite senatorial friends in Rome are cast as intermediaries to intercede with the emperor on the exiled poet's behalf. The enabling monarch who frees up his subjects' *otium* has become the disgruntled tyrant, whose displeasure becomes the task of their *negotium*. The epistolary framework of Ovid's *ex Ponto* presents a picture of Roman society at this time that is structured as a series of concentric circles, with the emperor placed at the centre. The senatorial elite are recast as courtiers, haunted by the political efficacy of their ancestors simply by virtue of the names they bear.[271]

Furthermore, within the *ex Ponto*, we are presented with explicit reminders of the constitutional system that continues to haunt the new era. In a number of poems in this collection, Ovid celebrates the news of the appointment of various friends and supporters to the consulship in Rome, and imagines

---

270   Furthermore, as with the ghosts of Marxism, the spectre of the Roman Republic that keeps returning in the imperial period has an economic dimension as well as a political one, insofar as one of the most tangible signifiers of the advent of monarchy in Rome was the use of the emperor's private fiscus (located and managed within his personal residence) as a major source of public expenditure to rival the state *aerarium*, which was located in the temple of Ops. Millar 1963 is still the seminal discussion of this shift. When Ovid famously comments at *Tr.* 4.4.15.16 that Caesar is the *res publica* (... *res est publica Caesar*), readers may be reminded of the newly privatised economic structures that the principate ushered in through the potential for *res* to mean 'property'.

271   The appearance of names that correspond with the names of known historical figures of the period is a function of the epistolary format of the *ex Ponto*. Cf. Nagle 1980, 77–82; and Oliensis 1997, 172–173 on the significant fact of these names after the coyness of the *Tristia*; and Syme 1978, 94–168 on the historical significance of the individuals named in the *ex Ponto* (which include both a Sextus Pompeius and a Paullus Fabius Maximus).

the scenes of their inauguration in a characteristic display of festal *enargeia*.[272] Yet, as Fergus Millar has highlighted, these poems are themselves an important witness to how much the consulship had changed in the new imperial age.[273] In *ex Ponto* 4.4, for example, where Ovid imagines the scene that will take place in Rome on January 1st, when his friend Sextus Pompeius will become consul for the ensuing year (14 CE), his account of the day's imagined ceremonies concludes with an image of the new consul giving thanks to the gods and Caesar, as if the consulship were now the emperor's gift.[274] In the following poem, which presents itself as a sequel to the imaginary events of *ex Ponto* 4.4, with Pompeius now imagined in office, Ovid concludes the list of consular duties that he envisages his friend undertaking with the image of him bringing the *princeps* and his heir the morning's customary salutation, as if the relationship between them were that of patron and client.[275]

The inauguration of Sextus Pompeius as consul has a hauntological significance that goes beyond the ghostly status of consular office at this time. The appointment of consuls takes place on a fixed date in the calendar, January 1st, and has a further significance for historical time because the names of the consuls for any given year will subsequently be used to identify that year for the historical record. Ovid's absence from the event of Pompeius' inauguration, and dependence upon unreliable rumour to discover whether or not the event has taken place, underscore the extent to which exile has displaced him from the structures of time that govern daily life in the city of Rome as well as those that would enable him to tell one year apart from another. This mode of temporal displacement, which is all the more striking for the comparison it inspires with Ovid's entry for January 1st in the *Fasti*,[276] produces a hauntological commentary on the interventions that Augustus was himself making into the fabric of Roman time in this period.[277] Removed from Rome, Ovid loses the certainty of knowing exactly when one year ends and another begins, thereby undermining the chronological certainty at which Augustus' calendar reforms' aim. But there is a more pointed comment underpinning the connection that Ovid draws in this poem between the uncertainty of knowing whether the

---

272   E.g. *ex P.* 4.4 and 4.9. Cf. Hardie 2002a, 313–315 for discussion of the vivid visualisations involved in the imagining of the scene of Sextus' consular inauguration in *ex P.* 4.4.

273   Millar 1993, 13–16.

274   *Ex P.* 4.4.39–40. Millar 1993, 14 notes the ambiguity of the object of this thanks.

275   *Ex P.* 4.3.23.

276   Although see Hardie 2002a, 315 n. 77 for the possibility that Ovid's entry for the corresponding episode of *Fasti* 1 might also have been revised in exile, a suggestion that amplifies the hauntological resonances of the scene in *ex P.* 4.4.

277   For discussion of these reforms, see Feeney 2007, 167–211.

new year has begun and the newfound meaninglessness that the consulship
accrues in this age of empire: it is as if time itself has become undifferentiated
with the emptying of consular office of any real meaning. For Roman subjects
living now, Ovid implies, all that matters is that they live in the age of Augustus,
and the years might as well roll by unmarked – an experiential reality that similarly undermines the busy industry of Augustus' calendar reforms.[278]

A refrain that crops up repeatedly in *Spectres of Marx* is the phrase uttered
by the ghost of Hamlet's father that 'time is out of joint.' Derrida uses this phrase
to articulate the damage done to the experience of time itself at moments of
historical disjunction, when a breach intervenes within the present so as to
make that present unavailable to the historical subject. The quality of untimeliness that descends at such moments is what lends them a spectral aura. In his
reformation of the Roman calendrical system, Augustus had created just such
a breach in historical time, insofar as he had reorganised the traditional ways
of measuring time at Rome, which had hitherto been anchored to the founding of the Republic, to orient them around himself.[279] But measuring time in
relation to the present cannot but have had a profoundly disorienting effect on
those contemporary subjects who were living *in* that Augustan present. Ovid's
description of time in the exile poetry offers a pointed commentary on this
new historical condition. Throughout his books of *exilica*, Ovid will characterise the experience of time on the edge of the Roman empire as radically different to the experience of time within the city of Rome, where festivals and other
religious, commercial and forensic activities served to distinguish the days
of the year apart from one another. In exile, time hangs heavily because the
seasons are undifferentiated (it seems to be permanently winter), and there
appear to be no urban activities available to tell one day apart from the next. If,
as Feeney once suggested, these books come to occupy the position in Ovid's

---

278   This idea resonates with a point made by Derrida 1994, 3: "Haunting is historical, to be
       sure, but it is not dated, it is never given a date in the chain of presents, day after day,
       according to the instituted order of a calendar. Untimely, it does not come to, it does not
       happen to, it does not befall, one day, Europe, as if the latter, at a certain moment of its
       history, had begun to suffer from a certain evil, to let itself be inhabited in its inside, that
       is, haunted by a foreign guest."

279   Feeney 2007, 172–182 on the significance of Augustus' interventions in the consular Fasti,
       where he supplements the list of consular names with periodic reminders of the number
       of years that have elapsed since the founding of the city by Romulus in 752 BCE (thereby
       generating an alternative measure of historical time to that charted by the republican
       institution of consuls); and also, from 22 BCE when Augustus stepped down from holding
       the consulship himself, by annotating the list of consuls for the year with the number of
       years since he had held *tribunicia potestas*.

literary career that the unwritten books of the *Fasti* should have taken,[280] then they underscore the difference between the experience of time in Rome and outside it. Or do they? For in this position they also proffer a pointed comment on the increasingly monotonous experience of time in the second half of the calendar, which Ovid refuses to complete, and which is, as scholars have suggested, disproportionately loaded with new festivals celebrating Augustus and the imperial family.[281] In lieu of the monotony of this calendar experience, Ovid offers an alternative monotonous experience of his own.

The sense of untimeliness that we experience in the exile poetry may be taken as a symptom of (or comment on) the ideological restructuring of time in this period, but it is also a consequence of Ovid's sustained reflection in exile on the effects and effectiveness of various kinds of media. This preoccupation is one that runs through his entire oeuvre from the very outset, as we have seen, but it takes centre stage in the poetry of exile, where distance from Rome confronts the poet with his profound reliance on media in order to communicate with a readership located so far away, and to learn about events taking place at a distance. Yet although this reliance may be an effect of his particular situation in exile, it takes on a broader significance for the new imperial age for which the exilic works present such an isolated witness, and for which 'exile' becomes, for later readers, an emblematic condition. The new political order is accompanied by a reorganization of the space of empire and by a newfound self-consciousness about its spatial expanse.[282] Its success is, moreover, premised on the imperial family's canny understanding of the power of media to convey the messages of imperial ideology across this expansive field.[283] Ovid's exile poetry taps into the novel media landscape of the early empire, and draws out the spectral implications of this landscape by highlighting the impact that these new media have on the disjointed temporal experience of senders and receivers, situated as they may be, like him, on different sides of a vast imperial map. As such, it resonates with a crucial aspect of Derrida's explication of hauntology in *Spectres of Marx*, which identifies

---

280 This is the argument of Feeney 1992.

281 On this, see Barchiesi 1997b, 199.

282 This point is made throughout Nicolet 1991 in his discussion of the significance of the map of Agrippa and its display in Rome. On this, see also Pandey 2018, 171.

283 Cf. Price 1984 on the spread of the imperial cult in Asia Minor; Martelli 2013, 197–202 on Ovid's references in exile to its pervasive reach in his own far-flung province in the form of household shrines and cult statues of the imperial family; and Pandey 2018, 231–232 on the effect that seeing cult statues, along with other media stamped with the emperor's image (e.g. coins), would have on viewers across the vast empire. Frampton 2019, 155–162 makes a similar point about the prevalence of imperial inscriptions in the late Augustan age.

the particular media apparatuses installed by late Capitalism as a factor that contributes significantly to the spectral quality of this era. It was precisely Derrida's focus on the role played by novel media forms that led the popular music industry to pick up this idea and use it to account for certain developments that they saw taking place in the industry since the 2010s. Their analyses of the relationship between the irruption of new (digital) media and the acceleration in the music industry's preoccupation with its own recent past, are worth a brief look for the insight that they may bring to our experiment in viewing Ovid's exile poetry as a comparable cultural product of a hauntological era.

In his work, Derrida had identified the development of new techno-tele-media apparatuses, and their properties of dislocation and acceleration, as a significant component of the spectral quality of political discourse at that moment – a prime example of a virtual agency that acts on events without existing in present space or time. The cultural hauntologists of the 2010s were drawn to Derrida's critique of these apparatuses because his objections to them presaged their own concerns about the impact that the internet had had more recently on the popular music industry.[284] Above all, Derrida's assessment of the impact that these apparatuses have had on our cultural and political moment highlights their effect of temporal displacement, and the quality of untimeliness that we experience in the present as present time is itself pushed aside by the pressure of the past and the promise of the future. For hauntological music critics, this temporal displacement has been exacerbated by the internet, which operates as a vast and readily accessible archive, and which has the effect of 'flattening' time, as it makes music from different historical eras equally available from the same, undifferentiated source. Yet for all that this displacement has a retrospective quality, these critics are also haunted by the future – more specifically, by the idea that the futures once promised for popular music by the new possibilities that technology and cultural pluralism should have made available had been lost or 'cancelled'.[285] They saw this manifested by the lack of interesting new sounds emerging in the post-internet age, and by pop's obsession not just with the songs of previous eras but with its sound production as well. This perceived lack then gave rise to new, deliberately hauntological genres of music, such as Vaporwave, which

---

284   *Spectres of Marx* was written before digital media had developed into the phenomena that they are today, yet Derrida's account of the spectral consequences of televisual media apparatuses for political and cultural discourse are uncannily prescient of the effects that new media have had on these discourses in our own time.

285   Cf. esp. Fisher 2014, 1–47 on 'lost futures.'

samples some of the most colourless sounds of recent pop music (e.g. elevator and lounge music – musical forms associated with the consumerist activities of late Capitalism) with the aim of satirising the consumerist reflexes of contemporary pop culture.[286] The distinctive melancholia of hauntological microgenres, such as Vaporwave, is further displayed in their habit of replicating the crackle of vinyl and of making this sonic materiality uncannily available via the distinctly immaterial modes of digital media.

Ovid's exile poetry is similarly haunted by both the past and the future in ways that resemble the current state of the music industry that Mark Fisher and other hauntologists describe. It is, as we have already seen, thoroughly backward-looking in its preoccupation with the recent past. Yet it is also haunted by the idea of lost futures: when we read this poetry, we cannot help but wonder what Ovid might have written at this stage in his career under different conditions – how he might have followed through on the promise of the *Metamorphoses'* innovations in an era of greater political freedom.[287] More than this, it actively cancels a literary future by bringing the history of Latin elegy, as a genre, to a close.[288] This is, I believe, a deliberate strategy, Ovid's way of inscribing this moment in the history of (lost) freedoms with the mark of cultural death. Neither erotic nor aetiological elegy would revive following Ovid's nine books of exile poetry, which perform the work of mourning for the very genre whose demise they effect. That they initially do so in a poetry collection (the *Tristia*) that explicitly takes elegy back to its origins in lament makes this work explicitly hauntological, a manifestation of Derrida's view of the apparition of ghosts as a movement that is both novel and repetitive, an advent and a return.[289] With the *Tristia* (and its follow-up collection, the *Ex Ponto*), Ovid 'haunts' Roman consciousness, returning to Rome as a ghost, a literary voice that is both strange and familiar at the same time.

---

286   Tanner 2016 offers a comprehensive account of the musical features, cultural meanings, and political message of the genre.

287   Labate 1987, 103–112 speculates that Ovid would have written the kind of occasional poetry that is later exemplified by Martial and Statius, and which we see glimpses of in Ovid's Triumph poems from exile (e.g. *Tr.* 4.2, and *ex P.* 2.1 and 3.4).

288   Cf. Fantham 2001, 206–211 for discussion of the closural significance of Ovid's exile poetry for Latin elegy as a genre. Fantham points to the absence of elegy from Statius' poetic oeuvre, and to the fact that when Martial writes in elegiac couplets, he calls these poems *epigrammata*, to make her case for the waning of elegy's star by the Flavian period, at least.

289   Derrida 1994, 10–11: "Repetition *and* first time: this is perhaps the question of the event as question of the ghost ... Repetition *and* first time, but also repetition *and* last time, since the singularity of any *first time* makes of it also a *last time*."

Much of the spectral quality of the *Tristia* and *Epistulae ex Ponto* is owed to the fact that Ovid's spatial distance from Rome produces a form of temporal distance as well, as a result of the delay imposed by the time it takes for the media he uses to cover the distance between Rome and Tomis. This is impressed in the opening poem of the *Tristia*, which describes the space separating Ovid from his Roman readers, by outlining the journey that his book-roll must undertake in order to make its way to Rome to deliver Ovid's poetry to his readership there. But this poem has the further task of demarcating the temporal disjunction between Ovid and his reader that this spatial divide conditions. *Tr.* 1.1 is an *envoi* poem, a poem that marks the end of the compositional process for the author, and which we expect to see last in a book of poems. Yet in *Tristia* 1, its author has placed it first, thereby ensuring that our temporal experience of reading this book is the reverse of its author writing it, as if to underscore the chronological inconcinnity between Ovid in Tomis and his reader in Rome. Ovid is thus absented from Rome in temporal as well as spatial terms, and explicitly marks the break of exile as one with chronological consequences. This inconcinnity is presented to us as an effect of the spatial and temporal dislocations produced by a particular textual medium – the book-roll – and thus anticipates Derrida's arguments about the kinds of temporal distortion produced by digital media apparatuses. This textual medium (the book-roll) was hardly new, but, writing from the periphery of the Roman world, Ovid had a novel vantage point from which to consider its capacity to distort space and time. His meditation in exile on the dislocations of the book-roll has further consequences for later readers like ourselves, who experience them to a different degree because of our removal from antiquity.

But the exilic works display the temporal disjunctions of hauntological media in another way as well, in the unusual degree of self-consciousness that they display about the materiality of the book-roll, the shabby appearance of which is described in programmatic and painstaking detail in *Tr.* 1.1.[290] Of course, the book-roll that Ovid describes bears no resemblance to the book-roll that his readers (even his earliest readers) will have actually read, which was the product of copying that took place in Rome, and was therefore unlikely to differ in appearance from other books being copied there. In drawing attention to the gap between the actual and fictive appearance of the book-roll,[291] Ovid undermines the illusion that the book we are reading is the book he was

---

290   Cf. Williams 1992 for an account of the tradition of book-roll poems that Ovid is reworking here.

291   This effect is seen, for example, in the mention of the *liturae* (made by the poet's tears) that are said to blot the pages of the text at *Tr.* 1.1.13.

writing, and thereby compromises any illusion we may harbour that the voice of the poet who speaks to us from these pages is in any vestigial sense present to us. In focusing our attention on the temporal disjunction between the fictive book and its material manifestation, Ovid produces for his readers something akin to the 'metaphysics of crackle' that is identified by Mark Fisher as a hallmark of hauntological genres of music.[292] With this phrase, Fisher describes the way in which the surface sound of an earlier recording medium (the crackle of vinyl, for example) is incorporated into digital music at the level of content. Fisher's description of this effect alludes to Derrida's account of the opposite illusion – the metaphysics of presence that is historically attributed to speech in the western philosophical tradition, and the concomitant assumption that any ideational original belongs to the spoken word. The incorporation of surface noise into the musical texture of a digital genre like Vaporwave disrupts this illusion of presence by deliberately reminding us that we are listening to a replica. Crackle allows listeners to hear that time is out of joint, and reminds them of the technological means by which this capturing – and rupturing – of time is made possible. Ovid's self-consciousness in the *Tristia* about the materiality of the *libellus* – the medium that enables him to communicate (or not) with those in Rome who may (or may not) be willing to listen – has an analogous effect.

In exile, Ovid was also in a position to experience and reflect on the distorting effects of other media that originated at Rome, some of which were destined to reach across the expanse of her newly reformed empire (monuments, statues and inscriptions, for example, could and did move as a result of processes of replication),[293] and some of which were not. The latter provide Ovid with some of his most fertile material for pointing up the chronological disjunction that opens up in the spatial distance separating Rome and Tomis. In a number of poems, for example, we see him anticipating news of a triumph

---

292 Cf. Fisher 2013. See also Fisher 2014, 21 for an eloquent description of the effect: "Crackle makes us aware that we are listening to a time that is out of joint; it won't allow us to fall into the illusion of presence. It reverses the normal order of listening according to which, as Ian Penman put it, we are habituated to the 're' of recording being repressed. We aren't only made aware that the sounds we are hearing are recorded, we are also made conscious of the playback systems we use to access the recordings."

293 Cf. Cooley 2006 on the movement of the RGDA, for example, across the province of Galatia; and Martelli 2010 on the relationship between this monumental inscription and Ovid's epitaph in *Tr.* 3.12, which moves in the opposite direction toward Rome. Frampton 2019, 155–162 contextualises the inscriptional references in Ovid's exile poetry further by plotting them against the broader step-change in Augustus' epigraphic habit that we witness toward the end of his regime. And cf. Pandey 2018, 232 on the replication and empire-wide circulation of imperial portraits on coins as well as statues.

in Rome.[294] When the news fails to reach him, Ovid proceeds to imagine the scene at Rome, inventing its content for himself as a substitute for actually being there, in a replay of a scene from the *Ars Amatoria* in which the would-be lover is told to invent answers to the questions of a curious girl as to what the various signs in the triumphal procession describe. As scholars have suggested, Ovid's games with triumphal semiotics both in the *Ars Amatoria* and in the exile poetry serve to highlight the fact that, as an institution, the triumph is always already a 'triumph' of representation over reality, insofar as it is charged with representing to Romans in Rome an event that happened far away. To make this event 'present' in Rome, the triumphal procession relies on a variety of representational devices – painted landscapes and written signs – to bring the object of the triumph (i.e. the defeated people or land) into Rome.[295] The ritual is therefore always one that takes place primarily 'in ink', and Ovid's written triumphs bring out a virtual logic that is integral to the triumph as a ritual practice.[296] Yet in writing these imaginary triumphs in exile, Ovid is doing something weirder for his Roman audience than he is even for himself, insofar as he delivers back to his readers in Rome an imaginary version of an event that they may have actually experienced (but which he himself has definitely not). The experience of reading these virtual triumphs on the page, and their misalignment with the readership's lived experience, may again be captured by the crackle effect that Mark Fisher describes for certain genres of digital music.

In exile, the triumph presents Ovid with a medium for reflecting on the untimeliness that is a condition of exile and, more broadly, of the new imperial subject, whether in or out of Rome. But his preoccupation with the Triumph is also a symptom of the increasing privatization of political power at this time in Rome, where the triumph had become, by this stage, the monopoly of the imperial family. Ovid's fixation with the triumph allows us to see the extent to which that family had moved into the centre of their imperial subjects' gaze, both at home and abroad. But if the imperial triumph affirms the

---

294   Ovid's preoccupation with an imperial triumph may be traced through *Tr.* 4.2, where he desires to hear news of an imperial conquest in Germany, and imagines the ensuing triumph in Rome; into *ex P.* 2.1, where report of an imperial triumph in Rome has reached Ovid in Tomis, and he proceeds to report its content; and then again in *ex P.* 3.4, in which he refers to a *Triumph* poem (assumed by scholars to be *ex P.* 2.1). Each of these poems builds (or plays) on the last one's games with triumphal representation.

295   As Hardie 2002a, 310 points out, the *triumphator*, who is cast as Jupiter for the duration of the triumph, occupies the same representational plane as the painted landscapes.

296   Cf. Hardie 2002a, 309–310; and Beard 2004. This argument also underpins much of Beard 2007. And see now Pandey 2018, 215–239.

Roman subject's role *as* subject (that is, as one subjected) to a new monarchical system of power, Ovid's take on this institution in exile is also a symptom
of his own complicity in a system of domination that sees the triumph as the
rightful privilege of the Roman over Rome's subject peoples. For in his poetry,
the triumph is always imagined in the eyes of its spectators in Rome, the audience who stood to gain from its display. This imperialist perspective is in keeping with other strategies at work in the exile poetry, which, as Tom Habinek
has cogently noted, serve to communicate to Rome's citizens the necessity of
the imperial project by representing to them the untamed, non-Roman world
against which Roman civilization is measured.[297] Ovid's depiction of the local
denizens of Tomis as trouser-wearing, spear-shaking, Getic-speaking barbar-
ians, is, as many scholars have noted, at odds with what the historical and
archaeological record tells us about this long-Hellenized city.[298] The palpable
exaggeration of his account of the local peoples, combined with his longing
for Rome, serves Rome's imperialist ideology, however much its reminder to
Romans of the extent to which the empire remained to be pacified might irk
individual members of the imperial family.

Habinek's critique of this imperialist agenda has the more pressing target of
critiquing those scholars who mark their own collusion with it by falling prey
to Ovid's own self-pitying self-portrait as a victim of the late-Augustan regime.
Scholars who sympathise with Ovid, or who set about demonstrating the strategies of resistance that one might attribute to his exile poetry, obscure the
broader imperialist logic in which his exilic laments are complicit. As Habinek
points out, confronting this logic is a challenge, since it goes against our 'natural' instinct to sympathise with the artist, especially one who is, as here, the victim of an intolerant monarch.[299] Yet such a response, on the part of both Ovid
and his critics, is at the expense of the subject peoples among whom Ovid finds
himself in exile, and whose non-Roman customs he deprecates.[300] To ignore
this aspect of exile's poetry is to succumb to Romanticist fantasies about
the apolitical innocence of literature from the ideological interests and

---

297   Habinek 1998, 151–152.
298   Habinek 1998, 158.
299   Habinek 1998, 164–169.
300   Habinek 1998, 158 notes in Ovid's fear of Getic customs (and particular horror of assimi-
       lating to their language and culture, as implied by the apparent absurdity in *ex P.* 4.13.25 ff.
       of his composition of a poem in Getic) a striking contrast with the New World encounters
       analysed by Greenblatt 1991, in which wonder constitutes the chief response. As Habinek
       points out, exiled to Tomis, the Roman poet casts himself as the chief wonder in his unfa-
       miliar environs.

assumptions of the elite Romans who produced it.[301] An easy trap to fall into, since, as Habinek eloquently puts it, 'this is exactly how literature works its ideological magic, by making us believe in the inevitability of its own enabling fictions.'[302]

Habinek's critique of Ovid's imperialist attitude towards the local Tomitans, and concomitant longing for Rome, is an important one. Yet it misses something, as a result of isolating Ovid's exile poetry from his preceding oeuvre. For as we have seen, the exile poetry marks a deliberate break from his earlier career, a break that bears a political message in and of itself. Ovid's attitude toward the foreigner forms a crucial part of this break. In the poetic works that precede the event of exile, Ovid had, after all, made a habit of voicing the subjectivities of alien and marginal figures. Throughout the *Metamorphoses*, for example, the narrative is focalised, more often than not, through the eyes of women, non-Romans (and non-Greeks), the enslaved and the monstrous. As we have seen, its focus on the categories of human/non-human has the political effect of casting the *Aeneid's* focus on Roman/non-Roman identities as provincial. And throughout the narrative, our sympathies are frequently aligned with the figures who choose various forms of alienation, including metamorphosis, over submission to a dominating power. However fictional these alien voices and figures may be, Ovid's realization of their imagined cognitive, emotional and somatic experiences is an important source of the epic poem's political charge. The absence of these voices from the exile poetry, and the reversal of perspective that we encounter in a literary landscape that privileges the voice of the Roman (Ovid), who speaks here *as* a Roman in a non-Roman world, presents a marked shift in literary practice.

To take this shift as a display of the author's true ideological colours, which are here 'revealed' under duress, would be to submit to the kind of biographical and/or intentionalist fallacy that Ovid's texts so often seem to invite. But it would also be to ignore the performative charge of another important feature of his exile poetry's commentary on the hauntological status of the late Augustan age. For Ovid's reversion in exile to the norms of Roman imperialist ideology can be seen as producing a significant 'lost future' for Latin poetry, which will never embrace (in ancient Roman culture, at least) the rich range of gendered, social, cultural and zoological identities that we see described in this author's pre-exilic works again. This transformation, which Ovid himself deliberately enacts in his oeuvre, resonates with a cultural move that Mark Fisher

---

301   An institutional habit of Classicists that Habinek 1998, 15–33 dissects, with particular reference to the figure of Basil Gildersleeve.

302   Habinek 1998, 167.

highlights about the lost futures of twentieth century music prior to the real-ization of the hauntological consequences of the Internet. Commenting on the propensity of earlier musicians, like David Bowie, to embrace alien identities, and thereby escape into other subjectivities and other worlds, Fisher writes: 'Identifying with the alien – not so much speaking for the alien, as letting the alien speak through you – was what gave 20th century popular music much of its political charge.'[303] As a genre like Vaporwave demonstrates, however, the artistic refusal of this process, like Ovid's reversion to the norms of Roman imperialist ideology in exile, may carry a political charge of its own.

7   Conclusion

For all the potential hazards of transmission (which, in Ovid's case, must include the real, if unrealized, threat of censorship), and for all the vicissitudes of his post-Classical reception, Ovid's poetry survives in greater bulk than that of any other Latin poet of his time and continues to be widely read. Indeed, the global reach of his popularity seems never to have been greater, as a number of recent conferences on the reception of Ovid in China attests.[304] That this is the case is thanks to procedures of canonization with which Classicists are all too familiar. Yet these procedures have now come under scrutiny, at the same time as Ovid's status as an author who should continue to be taught and read has also come into question. The exclusionary nature of the Classical canon (of which Ovid remains a pillar) has been called out by Costanze Güthenke and Brooke Holmes in their critique of the social, cultural, and racial limitations placed on our view of Greco-Roman antiquity by a canon constructed in the name of the Classical.[305] Ovid presents something of a paradox for this view of canonicity: on the one hand, he is an elite male Roman, whose literary por-trayals of violence against women have led to calls for his texts to be removed from curricula across university campuses in North America (and, no doubt, beyond). On the other, his work from exile casts him as the original author-on-the-margins, an object of social exclusion himself and inspiration for precisely

---

303   Fisher 2014, 42.

304   'Globalizing Ovid: An International Conference in Commemoration of the Bimillennium of Ovid's Death' took place at Shanghai Normal University, May 31st–June 2nd 2017. 'Ovid and Latin Classics in Chinese Translation' took place at Columbia Global Centers in Beijing, May 20th–24th 2019.

305   Güthenke and Holmes 2018.

those marginal voices that the field of Classics needs in order to diversify its understanding of culture, ancient and modern.[306]

Both the objections and the terms of recuperation that we might heap on Ovid in this vein are problematic in that they are each built on an assumed alignment between his status or identity and the meaning of his written works. The overwhelming number of stories in the *Metamorphoses* that focus on the rape of female figures are read by some as symptomatic of Ovid's own male subject position, and uncritical acceptance of violence against women as part of the status quo. Yet they might equally be read as a critique of that cultural norm. Likewise, the exile poetry may be disparaged or celebrated for the marginalised view that it offers of its author. But in some ways, each of these readings is as problematic as the other because both assume that the fundamental message of the exilic collections is biographical. However much we think we subscribe to the death of the author, the Ovidian author remains an especially compelling fiction, one that scholars have historically found very difficult to bracket off from appraisals of his work. Social status, the main weapon of cultural materialists, forms part of this biographical fiction. In this volume, I have attempted to get around this difficulty by situating Ovid's texts against various materialist forces that decentre the authorial, human subject from his assumed place at the centre of their meaning, while still allowing him sufficient autonomy to be able to comment on that process of displacement. The naturecultures that the *Metamorphoses* foregrounds evince the ecological consciousness of this 'pre-modern' text's broad social and cultural context, but still display the particular sensibility of its author toward such entanglements. While the media apparatuses and negative aesthetic choices that his exile poetry highlights are both a sign of the late-Augustan times and a deliberate comment on those times, one that spells out the effects of the newly consolidated regime on time, space and art.

A further paradox raised by any critique of Ovid's canonicity is that his oeuvre has provided an especially important channel for diversifying and queering the canon. The focus in the *Metamorphoses* on labile identities has proven particularly inspiring for writers interested in the fluidity of gender and sexual identities, and has provided an authorizing reference point for works written in this vein throughout the twentieth century and beyond, from Virginia Woolf's *Orlando* to the novels of Ali Smith.[307] So too for writers interested in

---

306   Most of the essays collected in Ingleheart 2011 focus on political exiles, rather than the socially marginalized, but Matzner 2011 is a notable exception.

307   Cf. Ranger 2019a for discussion of Smith's engagement with Ovid in three novels: *Like* (1997), *Girl Meets Boy* (2007), and *How To Be Both* (2014). On the topic of Smith's queer

transnational and/or transcultural identities: the *Metamorphoses* is one of the most important intertexts for Salman Rushdie's study of the immigrant experience in *The Satanic Verses*,[308] as also for the portrait of social, cultural, and racial plurality in early twentieth century New York in E.L. Doctorow's novel *Ragtime*.[309] Ovid's own canonicity provides an endorsement for works like these, helping to sanction their own entry into the canon and supporting their attempt to expand its parameters and diversify its outlook.

The materialist frameworks that I have outlined as new critical directions that scholarship on Ovid's poetry might take in the future suggest yet further ways of diversifying his canonical resonance. Ecocritical approaches to the *Metamorphoses*, for example, situate the poem within traditions of environmental writing that expand questions of identity beyond the human into wider zoological networks and relations. Ovid's place in these traditions is well-known to ecocritical scholarship on Renaissance literature.[310] But his enduring relevance to the environmental narratives of our own day is best illustrated by the conspicuous allusions to the *Metamorphoses* in Richard Powers' recent novel of human-tree relations, *The Overstory*.[311] The prominence of Ovid's voice in this contemporary novel of environmental endurance and decline demonstrates how far the ancient poet's ecological sensibility reaches into contemporary eco-fiction, spanning millennia of historical and environmental change to resonate with the deep predicament of our times.

Bibliography

Alaimo, S. (2010). *Bodily Natures: Science, Environment, and the Material Self*. Bloomington.

Allen, A.W. (1950). 'Sincerity and the Roman Elegists.' *CP* 45: 145–160.

Barad, K. (2007). *Meeting the Universe Halfway: Quantum Physics and the Entanglement of Matter and Meaning*. Durham, NC.

Barchiesi, A. (1986). 'Problemi d'interpretazione in Ovidio: continuità delle storie, continuazione dei testi.' *MD* 16: 77–107.

---

translation of Ovid in the latter novel, see also now Ranger 2019b.

308   Ziolkowski 2004, 173–176 on Rushdie's response to the *Metamorphoses* in *The Satanic Verses*.

309   Cf. Bevilacqua 1990, 105–106; and Roynon 2019 on the presence of the *Metamorphoses* in *Ragtime*.

310   The use that Shakespeare makes of Ovid's version of the Actaeon myth forms the centrepiece of Watson's seminal eco-critical reading of *As You Like It* in Watson 2006, 84–96.

311   Powers 2018.

Barchiesi, A. (1989). 'Voci e istanze narrative nelle *Metamorfosi* di Ovidio.' *MD* 23: 55–97.

Barchiesi, A. (1992). *Epistulae Heroidum 1–3*. Florence.

Barchiesi, A. (1993). 'Insegnare ad Augusto: Orazio Epistole 2.1 e Ovidio, Tristia II.' *MD* 31: 149–184.

Barchiesi, A. (1994a). Review of Spoth (1992). *A&R* 39: 111–112.

Barchiesi, A. (1994b). *Il Poeta e il Principe: Ovidio e il discorso augusteo*. Rome and Bari.

Barchiesi, A. (1995). Review of Hintermeier (1993). *JRS* 85: 325–327.

Barchiesi, A. (1997a). *The Poet and the Prince*. Berkeley and Los Angeles.

Barchiesi, A. (1997b). 'Endgames: Ovid's *Metamorphoses* 15 and *Fasti* 6.' In D. Roberts, F. Dunn, and D. Fowler (eds.), *Classical Closure: Reading the End in Greek and Latin Literature*. Princeton, 181–208.

Barchiesi, A. (1999). 'Vers une histoire à rebours de l'élégie latine: les Héroïdes doubles (16–21).' In A. Deremetz and J. Fabre Serris (eds.), *Élégie et Épopée dans la poésie ovidienne (Héroides et amours): En Hommage à Simone Viarre*. Lille, 53–67.

Barchiesi, A. (2001). *Speaking Volumes: Narrative and Intertext in Ovid and other Roman poets*. London.

Barchiesi, A. (2002). 'Narrative Technique and Narratology in the Metamorphoses.' In Hardie (ed.), 180–199.

Barkan, L. (1986). *The Gods Made Flesh: Metamorphosis and the Pursuit of Paganism*. New Haven.

Barthes, R. (1977). *Fragments d'un Discours Amoureux*. Paris.

Beard, M. (1987). 'A Complex of Times: No More Sheep on Romulus' Birthday.' *PCPS* 33: 1–15.

Beard, M. (2004). 'Writing Ritual: The Triumph of Ovid.' In A. Barchiesi, J. Rüpke, and S. Stephens (eds.), *Rituals in Ink*. Munich, 115–126.

Beard, M. (2007). *The Roman Triumph*. Cambridge, MA.

Bennett, J. (2004). 'The Force of Things: Steps toward an Ecology of Matter.' *Political Theory* 32.3: 347–372.

Bennett, J. (2010). *Vibrant Matter: A Political Ecology of Things*. Durham, NC.

Bessone, F. (1997). *P. Ovidii Nasonis Heroidum Epistula XII: Medea Iasoni*. Florence.

Bevilacqua (1990). 'Narration and History in E. L. Doctorow's Welcome to *Hard Times, The Book of Daniel*, and *Ragtime*.' *American Studies in Scandanavia* 22: 94–106.

Bianchi, E., Brill, S., and Homes, B. (eds.). (2019). *Antiquities Beyond Humanism*. Oxford and New York.

Boyd, B. (1997). *Ovid's Literary Loves: Influence and Innovation in the Amores*. Ann Arbor.

Braidotti, R. (2013). *The Posthuman*. Cambridge and Malden, MA.

Bretzigheimer, G. (2001). *Ovids Amores: Poetik in der Erotik*. Tübingen.

Brooks, P. (1992). *Body Work*. Cambridge, MA.

Bryant, L., Srnicek, N., and Harman, G. (eds.). (2011). *The Speculative Turn: Continental Materialism and Realism*. Melbourne.

Buell, L. (1998). 'Toxic Discourse.' *Critical Inquiry* 24.3: 639–665.

Bullard (1990). *Dumping in Dixie: Race, Class and Environmental Quality*. Abingdon.

Cahoon, L. (1988). 'The bed as battlefield: erotic conquest and military metaphor in Ovid's *Amores*.' *TAPA* 118: 293–307.

Carson, R. (1962). *The Silent Spring*. Cambridge, MA.

Casali, S. (1995a). 'Tragic Irony in Ovid, *Heroides* 9 and 11.' *CQ* 45: 505–511.

Casali, S. (1995b). 'Strategies of Tension (Ovid, *Heroides* 4). *PCPS* 42: 1–15.

Casali, S. (1995c). *P. Ovidii Nasonis Heroidum Epistula IX: Deianira Herculi*. Florence.

Chiu, A. (2016). *Ovid's Women of the Year: Narratives of Roman Identity in the Fasti*. Ann Arbor.

Cixous, H., and Clement, C. (1986). *The Newly Born Woman*. Manchester.

Clarke, B. (2008). *Posthuman Metamorphosis: Narrative and Systems*. New York.

Coleman, K. (1990). 'Fatal Charades: Roman executions staged as mythological enactments.' *JRS* 80: 44–73.

Cooley, A. (2006). *Res gestae divi Augusti: Text, Translation and Commentary*. Cambridge, UK.

Cronon, W. (ed.). (1995). *Uncommon Ground: Rethinking the Human Place in Nature*. New York.

Cronon, W. (1996). 'The Trouble with Wilderness: Or, Getting Back to the Wrong Nature.' *Environmental History* 1.1: 7–28.

Crutzen, P., and Stoermer, E. (2000). 'The "Anthropocene".' *IGBP Newsletter* 41.12.

Davis, P. (2006). *Ovid and Augustus: A Political Reading of Ovid's Erotic Poems*. London.

Derrida, J. (1967). *De la Grammatologie*. Paris.

Derrida, J. (1994). *Specters of Marx*. London and New York.

Derrida, J. (2002). 'The Animal that Therefore I Am (More to Follow) (trans. D. Wills).' *Critical Inquiry* 28.2: 369–418.

De Waal, F. (2001). *The Ape and the Sushi Master: Cultural Reflections by a Primatologist*. New York.

Dollimore, J. (1991). *Sexual Dissidence: Augustine to Wilde, Freud to Foucault*. Oxford.

Downing, E. (1990). 'Anti-pygmalion: the *praeceptor* in *Ars Amatoria*, Book 3.' *Helios* 17: 237–249.

Eagleton, T. (1996a). *Literary Theory: An Introduction*. Oxford.

Eagleton, T. (1996b). *The Illusions of Postmodernism*. Oxford.

Fantham, E. (2001). 'Roman Elegy: Problems of Self-Definition, and Redirections,' in *L'histoire Littéraire immanente dans la poésie latine*. Geneva.

Feeney, D. (1992). '*Si licet et fas est*: Ovid's *Fasti* and the problem of free speech under the Principate.' In A. Powell (ed.), 1–25.

Feeney, D. (1999). '*Mea tempora*: Patterning of time in the *Metamorphoses*.' In P. Hardie, A. Barchiesi, and S. Hinds (eds.), 13–30.

Feeney, D. (2007). *Caesar's Calendar: Ancient Time and the Beginnings of History*. Berkeley.

Feldherr, A. (2010). *Playing Gods: Ovid's Metamorphoses and the Politics of Fiction*. Princeton.

Fielding, I. (2017). *Transformations of Ovid in Late Antiquity*. Cambridge, UK.

Fisher, M. (2014). *Ghosts of My Life: Writings on Depression, Hauntology, and Lost Futures*. Alresford.

Fitton Brown, L. (1985). 'The Unreality of Ovid's Tomitan Exile.' *LCM* 10.18–22.

Fowler, D. (1999). 'Pyramus, Thisbe, King Kong: Ovid and the Presence of Poetry.' In D. Fowler (1999), *Roman Constructions*. Oxford.

Fowler, D. (forthcoming). *Unrolling the Text*.

Fragaszy, D., and Perry, S. (eds.). (2003). *The Biology of Traditions: Models and Evidence*. Cambridge, UK.

Frampton, S. (2019). *Empire of Letters: Writing in Roman Literature and Thought from Lucretius to Ovid*. Oxford and New York.

Franco, C. (2014). *Shameless: The Canine and the Feminine in Ancient Greece*. Berkeley.

Fränkel, H. (1945). *Ovid: A Poet Between Two Worlds*. Berkeley and Los Angeles.

Freud, S. (1922). 'The Medusa's Head.' In J. Strachey et al. (eds.), *The Standard Edition of the complete Psychological Works of Sigmund Freud (Vol. 18)*. London.

Fulkerson, L. (2005). *The Ovidian Heroine as Author: Reading, Writing, and Community in the Heroides*. Cambridge, UK.

Fulkerson, L. (2016). *Ovid: A Poet on the Margins*. London.

Gaertner, J.F. (2005). *Ovid Epistulae ex Ponto, Book 1*. Oxford.

Galasso, L. (1995). *P. Ovidii Nasonis Epistularum ex Ponto liber II*. Florence.

Gale, M. (1994). *Myth and Poetry in Lucretius*. Cambridge, UK.

Gasperoni (1996). 'The Unconscious is Structured Like a Language.' *Qui Parle* 9.2: 77–104.

Genette, G. (1997). *Palimpsests: Literature in the Second Degree*. Lincoln, NE.

Gibson, B. (1999). 'Ovid on Reading: Reading Ovid. Reception in Ovid, *Tristia* II.' *JRS* 89: 19–37.

Gibson, R. (2003). *Ovid: Ars Amatoria Book 3*. Cambridge, UK.

Gifford, T. (2016). 'The Environmental Humanities and the Pastoral Tradition.' In C. Schliephake (ed.), *The Ecocriticism, Ecology and the Cultures of Antiquity*. Lanham, MD.

Giusti, E. (2018). 'Tiresias, Ovid, and gender trouble: generic conversions from *Ars* into *Tristia*.' *Ramus* 47.1: 27–57.

Gowers, E. (2005). 'Talking Trees: Philemon and Baucis Revisited.' *Arethusa* 38.3: 331–365.

Gowers, E. (forthcoming). 'Are People really like Trees?'

Greenblatt, S. (1991). *Marvellous Possessions: The Wonder of the New World.* Chicago.

Greene, E. (1998). *The Erotics of Domination: Male Desire and the Mistress in Latin Love Poetry.* Baltimore.

Gregg, M., and Seigworth, G. (eds.). (2010). *The Affect Theory Reader.* Durham, NC.

Grosz, E. (1993). 'Bodies and Knowledges: Feminism and the Crisis of Reason.' In L. Alcoff and E. Potter (eds.), *Feminist Epistemologies.* London and New York.

Guha, R., and Martínez-Alier, J. (1997). *Varieties of Environmentalism: Essays North and South.* Abingdon.

Güthenke, C., and Holmes, B. (2018). 'Hyperinclusivity, Hypercanonicity, and the Future of the Field.' In M. Formisano and C. Kraus (eds.), *Marginality, Canonicity, Passion.* Oxford and New York.

Habinek, T. (1998). *The Politics of Latin Literature.* Princeton.

Hägglund, M. (2008). *Radical Atheism: Derrida and the Time of Life.* Palo Alto.

Hall, E. (2018). 'Materialisms Old and New.' In M. Telò and M. Mueller (eds.), *The Materialities of Greek Tragedy: Objects and Affect in Aeschylus, Sophocles, and Euripides.* London.

Haraway, D. (1985). 'A Cyborg Manifesto.' *Socialist Review* 80: 65–108.

Haraway, D. (2003). *The Companion Species Manifesto: Dogs, People, and Significant Otherness.* Chicago.

Haraway, D. (2010). *Staying with the Trouble: Making Kin in the Chthulucene.* Durham, NC.

Hardie, P. (1988). 'Lucretius and the Delusions of Narcissus.' *MD* 20–21: 71–89.

Hardie, P. (1990). 'Ovid's Theban History: the first "anti-Aeneid?".' *CQ* 40.1: 224–235.

Hardie, P. (2002a). *Ovid's Poetics of Illusion.* Cambridge, UK.

Hardie, P. (ed.). (2002b). *The Cambridge Companion to Ovid.* Cambridge, UK.

Hardie, P., Barchiesi, A., and Hinds, S. (eds.). (1999). *Ovidian Transformations: Essays on the Metamorphoses and its Reception.* *PCPS* Suppl. 23.

Harman, G. (2002). *Tool-Being: Heidegger and the Metaphysics of Objects.* Peru, IL.

Harman, G. (2018). *Object-Oriented Ontology: A New Theory of Everything.* London.

Harries, B. (1989). 'Causation and the Authority of the Poet in Ovid's *Fasti*.' *CQ* 39.1: 164–85.

Harries, B. (1991). 'Ovid and the Fabii: *Fasti* 2.193–474.' *CQ* 41.1: 150–168.

Hayles, K. (1999). *How We Became Posthuman: Virtual Bodies in Cybernetics, Literature, and Informatics.* Chicago and London.

Heinze, R. (1919). *Ovids elegische Erzählung.* Leipzig.

Heise, U. (2016). *Imagining Extinction: The Cultural Meanings of Endangered Species.* Chicago.

Henderson, J. (1997). 'Not wavering but frowning: Ovid as isopleth (*Tristia* 1 through 10).' In G. Williams and A. Walker (eds.), 139–171.

Hinds, S. (1998). *Allusion and Intertext: dynamics of appropriation in Roman poetry.* Cambridge, UK.

Hinds, S. (1987b). *The Metamorphosis of Persephone: Ovid and the self-conscious muse.* Cambridge, UK.

Hinds, S. (1992). 'Arma in Ovid's *Fasti* (Parts 1 and 2).' *Arethusa* 25.1: 81–153.

Hinds, S. (1999a). 'After exile: time and teleology from *Metamorphoses* to *Ibis.*' In P. Hardie, A. Barchiesi, and S. Hinds (eds.), (1999), 48–67.

Hinds, S. (1999b). 'First among women: Ovid, *Tristia* 1.6 and the traditions of 'exemplary' Catalogue.' *PCPhS Suppl.* 22, 123–142. Cambridge, UK.

Hinds, S. (2002). 'Landscape with Figures: Aesthetics of Place in the *Metamorphoses* and its Tradition.' In P. Hardie (ed.), 122–149.

Holmes, B. (2015). 'Situating Scamander: 'Natureculture' in the *Iliad.*' *Ramus* 44.1–2: 29–51.

Holzberg, N. (1997). *Ovid: Dichter und Werk.* Munich.

Holzberg, N. (2018). 'Gli *Amores* di Ovidio negli studi in lingua inglese del 2003–2016: la filologia classica nella sua *Splendid Isolation.*' In P. Fedeli and G. Rosati (eds.), *Ovidio 2017: Prospettive per il terzo millennio.* Teramo, 91–108.

Hopkinson, N. (2000). *Ovid: Metamorphoses Book XIII.* Cambridge, UK.

Ingleheart, J. (2006). 'What the poet saw: Ovid, the error, and the theme of sight in *Tristia* 2.' *MD* 56.1: 63–86.

Ingleheart, J. (ed.). (2011). *Two Thousand Years of Solitude: Exile after Ovid.* Oxford.

Iovino, S., and Opperman, S. (2014). *Material Ecocriticism: Materiality, Agency, and Models of Narrativity.* Bloomington.

James, S. (2003). *Learned Girls and Male Persuasion: Gender and Reading in Roman Love Elegy.* Berkeley and Los Angeles.

Jameson, F. (1991). *Postmodernism, or, the Cultural Logic of Late Capitalism.* Durham, NC.

Janan, M. (1994). *"When the Lamp is Shattered": Desire and Narrative in Catullus.* Carbondale and Edwardsville.

Keith, A. (1994). '*Corpus eroticum*: elegiac poetics and elegiac *puellae* in Ovid's *Amores.*' *CW* 88: 27–40.

Kennedy, D. (1992). '"Augustan" and "anti-Augustan": Reflections on Terms of Reference.' In A. Powell (ed.), 26–58.

Kennedy, D. (1993). *The Arts of Love: Five Studies in the Discourse of Roman Love Elegy.* Cambridge, UK.

Kennedy, D. (2012). 'Loves Tropes and Figures.' In B. Gold (ed.), *A Companion to Roman Love Elegy.* Malden, MA and Oxford.

Kenney, E. (1965). 'The Poetry of Ovid's Exile.' *PCPS* 11: 37–49.

Kenney, E. (1996). *Ovid, Heroides 16–21.* Cambridge, UK.

Kenney, E. (2001). Review of Bretzigheimer (2001). *BMCR* 2001.10.39.

Knox, P. (ed.). (1995). *Ovid, Heroides: Select Epistles*. Cambridge, UK.

Krasne, D. (2012). 'The Pedant's Curse: Obscurity and Identity in Ovid's *Ibis*.' *Dictynna* 9.

Krasne, D. (2016). 'Crippling Nostalgia: *Nostos*, Poetics and the Structure of the *Ibis*.' *TAPA* 46.1: 149–189.

Kristeva, J. (1981). *Desire in Language*. New York.

Kristeva, J. (1984). *Revolution in Poetic Language* (trans. M. Waller). New York.

Kyriakidis, S., and De Martino, F. (2004). *Middles in Latin Poetry*. Bari.

Labate, M. (1984). *L'Arte di Farsi Amare: Modelli culturali e progetto didascalico nell'elegia ovidiana*. Pisa.

Labate, M. (1987). 'Elegia triste ed elegia liete: Un caso di riconversione letteraria.' *MD* 19: 91–129.

Lacan, J. (1998). *Encore: The Seminar of Jacques Lacan XX (On Feminine Sexuality, the Limits of Love and Knowledge)* (trans. B. Fink). New York.

Lacan, J. (2006). *Écrits* (trans. Bruce Fink). New York.

Latour, B. (1987). *Science in Action: How to Follow Scientists and Engineers through Society*. Cambridge, MA.

Latour, B. (1993). *We Have Never Been Modern* (trans. C. Porter). Cambridge, MA.

Latour, B. (2005). *Reassembling the Social: an introduction to actor-network theory*. Oxford and New York.

Latour, B. (2017). *Facing Gaia: Eight Lectures on the New Climatic Regime*. Cambridge, UK.

Lindheim, S. (2003). *Mail and Female: Epistolary Narrative and Desire in Ovid's Heroides*. Madison, WI.

Luhmann, N. (1995). *Social Systems*. Palo Alto.

Martelli, F. (2010). 'Signatures, Events, Contexts: Copyright at the End of the First Principate.' *Ramus* 39.2: 130–159.

Martelli, F. (2013). *Ovid's Revisions: The Editor as Author*. Cambridge, UK.

Martindale, C. (1988). *Ovid Renewed. Ovidian Influences on Literature and Art from the Middle Ages to the Twentieth Century*. Cambridge, UK.

Marx, L. (2008). 'The Idea of Nature in America.' *Daedalus* 137.2: 8–21.

Matzner, S. (2011). 'Tomis writes back: Politics of peripheral identity in David Malouf's and Vintila Horrian's Re-narrations of Ovidian Exile.' In J. Ingleheart (ed.), 307–324.

McKibben, B. (1989). *The End of Nature*. London.

Millar, F. (1963). 'The Fiscus in the First Two Centuries.' *JRS* 53: 29–42.

Millar, F. (1993). 'Ovid and the *Domus Augusta*: Rome see from Tomoi.' *JRS* 83: 1–17.

Miller, J. (1994). 'Apostrophe, Aside, and the Didactic Addressee: Poetic Strategies in *Ars Amatoria* III.' *MD* 31: 231–241.

Morgan, K. (1977). *Ovid's Art of Imitation: Propertius in the Amores*. Leiden.

Morton, T. (2007). *Ecology without Nature*. Cambridge, MA.

Morton, T. (2013). *Hyperobjects: Philosophy and Ecology after the End of the World*. Minneapolis.

Murgia, C.E. (1985). 'Imitation and authenticity in Ovid's *Metamorphoses* 1.477 and *Heroides* 15.' *AJP* 106: 456–474.

Myerowitz, M. (1985). *Ovid's Games of Love*. Detroit.

Myers, S. (1994). *Ovid's Causes: Cosmology and Aetiology in Ovid's Metamorphoses*. Ann Arbor.

Myers, S. (1999). 'The Metamorphosis of a Poet: Recent Work on Ovid.' *JRS* 89: 190–204.

Nagle, B. (1980). *The Poetics of Exile: Program and Polemic in the Tristia and Epistulae ex Ponto of Ovid*. Brussels.

Nersessian, A. (2017). 'What is the New Redistribution?' *PMLA* 132.5: 1220–1225.

Newlands, C. (1995). *Playing with Time: Ovid and the Fasti*. Ithaca, NY.

Nicolet, C. (1991). *Space, Geography, and Politics in the Early Roman Empire*. Ann Arbor.

Nixon, R. (2011). *Slow Violence: Environmentalism of the Poor*. Cambridge, MA.

Oliensis, E. (1997). 'Return to sender: the rhetoric of *nomina* in Ovid's *Tristia*.' In G. Williams and A. Waler (eds.), 172–193.

Oliensis, E. (2009). *Freud's Rome: Psychoanalysis and Latin Poetry*. Cambridge, UK.

Oliensis, E. (2019). *Loving Writing/Ovid's* Amores. Cambridge, UK.

O'Rourke, D. (2018). 'Make War Not Love: *Militia Amoris* and Domestic Violence in Roman Elegy.' M. Gale, M., and Scourfield, D. (eds.), *Texts and Violence in the Roman World*. Cambridge, UK.

Otis, B. (1970). *Ovid as an Epic Poet*. Cambridge, UK.

Pandey, N. (2018). *The Poetics of Power in Augustan Rome. Latin Poetic Responses to Early Imperial Iconography*. Cambridge, UK.

Parry, H. (1966). 'Ovid's *Metamorphoses*: Violence in a Pastoral Landscape.' *TAPA* 95: 268–282.

Pasco-Pranger, M. (2006). *Founding the Year: Ovid's Fasti and the Poetics of the Roman Calendar*. Leiden.

Patin, M. (1868). *Études sur la poésie latine*, Vol. 1. Paris.

Plumwood, V. (1993). *Feminism and the Mastery of Nature*. London and New York.

Plumwood, V. (2002). *Environmental Culture: The Ecological Crisis of Reason*. Abingdon and New York.

Porter, J. (2016). *The Sublime in Antiquity*. Cambridge, UK.

Porter, J. (2019). 'Hyperobjects, OOO, and the Eruptive Classics.' In Bianchi, Brill, and Holmes (eds.), 189–210.

Powell, A. (ed.). (1998). *Roman Poetry and Propaganda in the Age of Augustus*. London.

Price, S. (1984). *Rituals and Power: The Roman Imperial Cult in Asia Minor*. Cambridge, UK.

Ranger, H. (2019a). 'Ali Smith and Ovid.' In T. Roynon and D. Orrells (eds.), 397–416.

Ranger, H. (2019b). '"Reader, I married him/her": Ali Smith, Ovid, and Queer translation.' *CRJ* 11.3: 231–255.

Redfield, J. (1975). *Nature and Culture in the Iliad: The Tragedy of Hector*. Chicago.

Reynolds, S. (2011). *Retromania: Pop Culture's addiction to its own past*. London.

Richlin, A. (2014). *Arguments with Silence: Writing the History of Roman Women*. Ann Arbor.

Rimell, V. (2006). *Ovid's Lovers*. Cambridge, UK.

Rimell, V. (2019). 'After Ovid, After Theory.' In T. Roynon and D. Orrells (eds.), 446–469.

Rosati, G. (1983). *Narciso e Pigmalione: Illusione e spettacolo nelle Metamorfosi di Ovidio*. Pisa.

Rosati, G. (1992). 'L'elegia al femminile: le *Heroides* di Ovidio (e altre heroides).' *MD* 29: 71–94.

Rosati, G. (1996). *P. Ovidii Nasonis Heroidum Epistulae XVIII–XIX*. Florence.

Roynon, T. (2019). 'Ovid, Race, and Identity in E. L. Doctorow's *Ragtime* (1975) and Jeffrey Eugenides' *Middlesex* (2002).' In T. Roynon and D. Orrells (eds.), 377–396.

Roynon, T., and Orrells, D. (2019). *Ovid and Identity in the Twenty-first Century. International Journal of the Classical Tradition* 26.

Ruddiman. (2003). 'The Anthropogenic Greenhouse Era began Thousands of Years Ago.' *Climatic Change* 61: 261–293.

Saussure, F. (1983). *Course in General Linguistics* (trans. R. Harris). London.

Schiesaro, A. (2011). 'Ibis, Redibis.' *MD* 67 79–150.

Schiesaro, A. (2014). '*Materiam superabat opus*: Lucretius metamorphosed.' *JRS* 104: 73–104.

Schwindt, J. (2016). *Thaumatographia oder Zur Kritik der philologischen Vernunft*. Heidelberg.

Segal, C. (1981). *Tragedy and Civilization: an Interpretation of Sophocles*. Norman, OK.

Segal, C. (1969). *Landscape in Ovid's Metamorphoses: A Study in the Transformation of a Literary Symbol*. Wiesbaden.

Serres, M. (1977). *La naissance de la physique dans le texte de Lucrèce: Fleuves et turbulences*. Paris.

Sissa, G. (2019). 'Apples and poplars, nuts and bulls: The poetic biosphere of Ovid's *Metamorphoses*.' In E. Bianchi, S. Brill, and B. Holmes (eds.), *Antiquities Beyond Humanism*. Oxford.

Slocombe, W. (2005). 'Littered with meaning: the problem of sign pollution in postmodern, post-structuralist, and ecocritical thought.' *Textual Practice* 19.4: 493–508.

Soper, K. (1995). *What is Nature? Culture, Politics and the Non-human*. Oxford.

Spentzou, E. (2003). *Readers and Writers in Ovid's Heroides: Transgressions of Genre and Gender*. Oxford and New York.

Spivak, G. (1988). 'Can the Subaltern Speak?' In C. Nelson and L. Grossberg (eds.), *Marxism and the Interpretation of Culture*. London.

Strathern, M. (1991). *Partial Connections*. Lanham, MD and Oxford.

Syme, R. (1978). *History in Ovid*. Oxford.

Tanner, G. (2016). *Babbling Corpse: Vaporwave and the Commodification of Ghosts*. Alresford.

Tarrant, R.J. (1981). 'The authenticity of the letter from Sappho to Phaon (*Heroides* XV).' *HSCP* 85: 133–153.

Thompson, C. (2005). *Making Parents: The Ontological Choreography of Reproductive Technologies*. Cambridge, MA.

Thorsen, T. (2014). *Ovid's Early Poetry: From his Single Heroides to his Remedia Amoris*. Cambridge, UK.

Tissol, G. (1997). *The Face of Nature: Wit Narrative and Cosmic Origins*. Princeton.

Tissol, G. (2014). *Ovid: Epistulae ex Ponto, Book 1*. Cambridge, UK.

Tutrone, F. (2020). 'Coming to know Epicurus' Truth: distributed cognition in Lucretius' *De Rerum Natura*.' In D. O'Rourke (ed.), *Approaches to Lucretius*. Cambridge, UK.

Vance, N. (1988). 'Ovid and the Nineteenth Century.' In Martindale (ed.), (1988), 215–232.

Vernant, and Vidal-Naquet, P. (1972). *Mythe et Tragédie en Grèce Ancienne*. Paris.

Verran, H. (2001). *Science and an African Logic*. Chicago.

Watson, R. (2006). *Back to Nature: The Green and the Real in the Late Renaissance*. Philadelphia.

Weiskel, T. (1976). *The Romantic Sublime: Studies in the Structure and Psychology of Transcendence*. Baltimore and London.

Wheeler, S. (1999). *A Discourse of Wonders: Audience and Performance in Ovid's Metamorphoses*. Philadelphia.

Wheeler, S. (2000). *Narrative Dynamics in Ovid's Metamorphoses*. Tübingen.

Whitehead, A. (1929). *Process and Reality*. New York.

Williams, R. (1976). *Keywords: A Vocabulary of Culture and Society*. London.

Williams, G. (1992). 'Representations of the Book-roll in Latin poetry: *Tr.* 1.1.3–14 and related texts.' *Mnemosyne* 45: 178–189.

Williams, G. (1994). *Banished Voices: Readings in Ovid's exile poetry*. Cambridge, UK.

Williams, G. (1996). *The Curse of Exile: A Study of Ovid's Ibis*. PCPhS Suppl. 19. Cambridge, UK.

Williams, G., and Walker, A. (eds.). (1997). *Ovid and Exile* (2 Vols.). *Ramus* 26.1 and 26.2.

Wolfe, C. (2010). *What is Posthumanism?* Minneapolis and London.

Wyke, M. (1987a). 'Written Women: Propertius' *Scripta Puella*.' *JRS* 77: 47–61.

Wyke, M. (1987b). 'The Elegiac Woman at Rome.' *PCPS* 33: 153–178.

Wyke, M. (1989a). 'Mistress and Metaphor in Augustan Elegy.' *Helios* 16.1: 25–47.

Wyke, M. (1989b). 'Reading Female Flesh: *Amores* 3.1.' In A. Cameron (ed.), *History as Text*. London, 113–143.

Wyke, M. (2002). *The Roman Mistress: Ancient and Modern Representations*. Oxford and New York.

Ziolkowski, T. (2004). *Ovid and the Moderns*. Ithaca, NY.

Zissos, A., and Gildenhard, I. (1999). 'Problems of Time in *Metamorphoses* 2.' In P. Hardie, A. Barchiesi and S. Hinds (eds.), 31–47.

Zuckerberg, D. (2018). *Not All Dead White Men: Classics and Misogyny in the Digital Age*. Cambridge, MA.